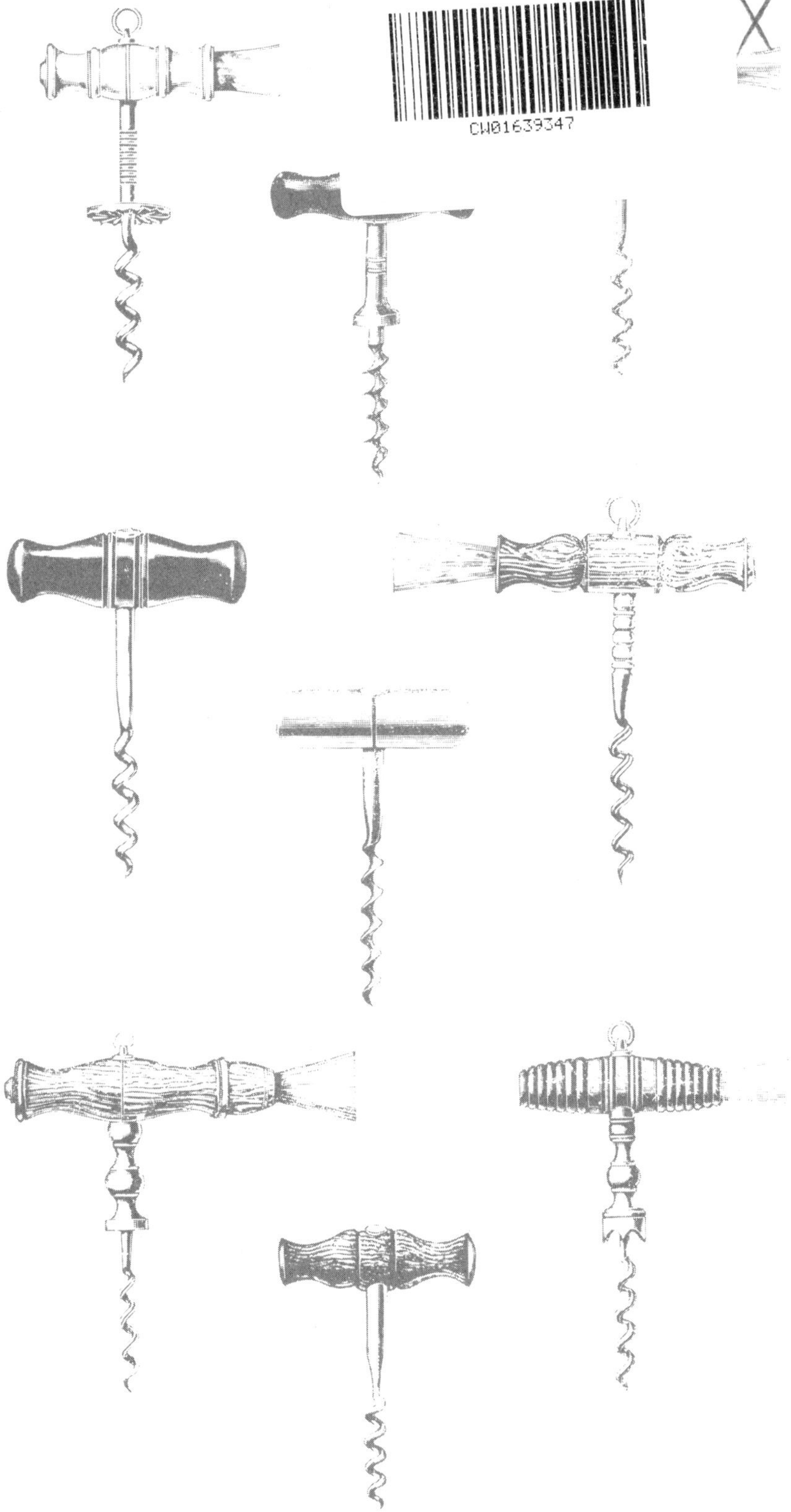

# MAKING SENSE *of* WINE TASTING

# MAKING SENSE *of* WINE TASTING

ALAN YOUNG

*Lennard Publishing*
*1 9 8 7*

Lennard Publishing
a division of Lennard Books Ltd
The Old School, Brewhouse Hill
Wheathampstead, Herts AL4 8AN

British Library Cataloguing in Publication Data
Young, Alan, 1927 –
Making sense of wine tasting.
1. Wine tasting
I. Title
641.2'2 TP548.5.A5

ISBN 1 85291 011 9

First published in Australia by
Greenhouse Publications Pty Ltd
385 Bridge Road
Richmond Australia 3121
1986
First Published in Great Britain 1987



Designed by Pocknell & Co
Printed and bound in England

# CONTENTS

From the typing of the first draft to the final editing of finished manuscript, many women have made generous contributions to this book. I can think of nothing more fitting than to dedicate the work to the women winelovers of the world; one in particular, Helen, for all her generosity, warmth and friendship.

# INTRODUCTION

Not only does one drink wine,
but one inhales it, looks at it, tastes it —
and then talks about it.

EDWARD VII

Winemaking is very much like painting. The appreciation of painting is either subjective, 'I don't know much about art but I know what I like' or objective, based on some genuine knowledge of what the artist is trying to convey. It is this latter kind that leads us to deeper and more subtle levels of understanding. As in any other field of human endeavour, knowledge opens up new horizons.

Winemakers, like painters, start with a range of basic materials; soil, grapes, climate. Yet these essential elements can change dramatically in less than a mile, let alone across nations or oceans. A cabernet grape, for example, grown in New York State, near the Canadian border, or on the island of Tasmania, will provide very different flavours from the same variety grown in the warmer climes of Algeria or Texas. Add to this the variables of the winemaker's art – whether to pick grapes earlier or later, use $SO_2$ or not, leave the 'must' on skins longer or shorter, whether to ferment the wine in barrels. The possibilities are endless . . . Then there is the range of equipment; irrigation systems, fermentation tanks of wood, stainless steel and concrete, centrifuges, diatomaceous earth filters, tank presses, vertical drainers . . . Here too the possibilities are endless.

It's only necessary for the winelover to tour the Barossa or Napa Valleys, Rioja, Bordeaux or Alba noting the amazing variations of equipment being used by winemakers to achieve a common end, to understand why wines are so different. We've come a long way from the old Bacchanalian treading of the harvest.

For a full appreciation of wine we need to know something about all these things just as the art lover extends his response to art by understanding the varying elements that create it. Above all we need to know something about how our senses guide us in the appreciation of wine or food.

Most of what we know about the world around us we learn from our senses. Despite enormous advances in scientific knowledge, technology and chemical analysis over the past half century, wine can still only be properly assessed by human sensory evaluations, i.e. sight, hearing, smell, touch and taste – as variable as this is from one person to another. In any exhibition wine is judged by humans, not by machines.

This, of course, leaves the door open to the charlatan, whether he be the winemaker charging exorbitant prices for poor quality in the hope that the lofty price tag will impress, or the wine snob who summarily condemns new wine styles, or wine from certain areas, producers or processes. One should always be wary of the 'knocker' who goes in for generalised judgements, 'Irrigated areas can't produce good table wines', or, 'Only French wines are worth tasting' and the 'expert' who can't justify his judgement in specific language: 'It's a naive domestic Burgundy without any breeding, but I think you'll be amused by its presumption.' (Thanks, James Thurber!)

The human element in sensory evaluation also leaves the door open to simple relativism – the idea that, because our senses are subjective, one person's opinion is as good as the next and there can be no objective judgement at all. It's the 'I don't know much about art but I know what I like' theory applied to wine. Certainly no wine critic or winemaker can talk about quality in relation to your own taste; if you taste a wine as bitter, then it *is* bitter. And certainly wine can be enjoyed by anyone, even those who know nothing of its components. A quality wine can be defined generally as one free of measurable faults and one that gives us pleasure; a wine either gives us pleasure, or it does not – regardless of what others may say or think.

But we should be aware at the outset that our concept of quality has much to do with our habits and upbringing, with products with which we are familiar or comfortable. With wine, habit tends to lead us to wellknown brands and familiar tastes. Of course, there is a positive place for the well promoted label. In most cases, these are carefully researched 'popular' tastes that will not offend, that are reliable, inexpensive and likely to win people over to wine. In fact, such *vins de table* styles are the wines most of us drink with our everyday meals. Not even the most ardent wine-lovers want to drink champagne and eat caviar every time they sit down to dinner. Nor could they afford to. And this brings up another determining factor on quality – price.

Much potential appreciation of wine is killed by sheer monetary consideration, some winelovers just cannot afford expensive wines. To produce high quality distinctive wines requires expensive grapes – cabernet, riesling, chardonnay, sauvignon blanc, etc – and for the red wines (and some whites) lots of new oak casks costing a small fortune. Such wines must command premium prices, although there is probably less difference between average and top class wines in South America, Australia, Italy and, to a lesser extent, the USA than other wine producing nations. While this situation lasts (and that won't be for long) we have an excellent chance to develop skill and judgement in wine evaluation and appreciation. The traditional 'goodies' from France and Germany have gone through the price ceiling for most of us not on expense accounts. This means that we turn our attention to the undiscovered delights of Argentina, South Africa, Italy, Spain, the unfashionable and lesser 'growths'. Be adventurous in your wine purchases. Try those 'strange' labels from New York State, Piedmont, La Mancha or Western Australia. That way you will obtain maximum pleasure from this work and, maybe, you will discover some unknown great wines. I do regularly.

And it's here that the challenge of learning how to appraise wines, understand new flavours, varieties, treatments, is worthwhile; the search for quality at an affordable price. While the axiom 'you get what you pay for' may still be largely true ('though I'm afraid price no longer necessarily equates with quality), and while it is common for the uninitiated to make positive responses to expensive wines, they could generally obtain equal pleasure from an unknown £3 wine. Some price snobs may decide the quality of the wine when they see the £3 sticker. Chances are that their assessment would be different if they tasted the wine before seeing the price. Then a 'bad' wine may be assessed as 'good value' or a 'bargain' with the wine being tasted on its merits, rather than the price dictating the assessment.

For the proper training of our sensory perceptions in regard to wine, three things are necessary. Firstly, knowledge about how our various senses respond, and how wine appeals to them. That knowledge is the basic concern of this book. Secondly, the development of a disciplined concentration which can identify minute traces of chemical substances and a host of other wine components, and a memory that will recall taste and odour characteristics. These two are interrelated; inability to concentrate will quickly kill the memory. It is for this reason that most professional wine judgements are made early in the day when our senses are sharpest and we are less liable to interruptions. Fatigue, noise, flashing lights, highly perfumed flowers (or women) and other distractions are not conducive to objective evaluation.

Thirdly, the use of precise language. It is often difficult to relate to terms in which wine is described – cuddly, elegant, delicate, cheeky, pretentious, foul, etc – which are so personal and so vague that they are virtually meaningless. Yet no-one can tell what is good or bad about a wine until he or she can put a name to it. When names describe objective qualities of wine it then becomes possible for one person to communicate his or her experiences to another, and the learning process is hastened and enjoyed.

During your study of this text you will notice that the words taste, flavour, touch, palate and sweetness, in particular, come under close scrutiny. Over the years, these absolutely fundamental words of sensory appraisal have been brought into common usage somewhat removed from their real meanings as we know them today.

Now is a good time to set the record straight. While some people will have difficulty adjusting, I'm proposing that these words be carefully examined and then used in their correct context for sensory evaulation.

# QUALITY

Quality is an intellectual phenomenon
that occurs between the wine and the taster;
it is independently related to neither.

RICHARD NELSON, PhD, CANADA

# DEFINING QUALITY

At seminars around the world many winelovers are astonished when asked to define quality. But, until we each determine our own concept of quality it is extremely difficult, if not impossible, to make an evaluation – sensory or otherwise – of anything. Few people can verbalise their opinion of quality, as ridiculous as this sound. Can you?

What is a quality restaurant (as opposed to a pretentious restaurant), a quality automobile, suit of clothes, wine, meal? Or quality anything? And who sets the standards for quality?

Let's look at an obvious source – Webster's Dictionary – for the answer:

1. A characteristic or attribute of something: property; a feature.
2. The natural or essential character of something.
3. Excellence; superiority.
4. Degree or grade of excellence.
5. (a) A high social position.
   (b) People of high social positions.

Frankly, none of these come anywhere near my concept of quality, and, if you check a selection of those submitted by winelovers who have attended my courses around the world you'll possibly agree that Dr Richard Nelson's definition is incredibly accurate: 'Quality is an intellectual phenomenon that occurs between the wine and the taster.'

Here's what some of my students have to say about the subject:

1. A standard of acceptance at my current level of development.
2. An objective standard of excellence, with an absence of technical faults.
3. A measurement of the extent to which an item satisfies one of the senses.

Most people would agree that quality is a double-sided coin – quality should have both physical and psychological attributes.

## WITHOUT FAULT

Nearly all physical commodities – wine, clothing, automobiles, furniture etc, are made to a set of standard specifications enabling us to measure whether the product is free of measurable faults. A surprising number of students consider that a quality article *may* have a measurable fault. Part of the appeal of handmade furniture or pottery, one might say, is the irregularity that proclaims the hand of its maker. Yet this isn't a virtue we'd seek in other products – a car, food or clothes. For my money, a wine (or any other product) wearing an expensive price tag must be faultless to earn quality recognition.

## ANTICIPATION AND EXPECTATION

The psychological aspect of quality rests in anticipation and expectation. We preset standards for almost any activity in which we participate; if the event or product lives up to our expectations it's fairly sure that we will give it top quality rating.

Dr Ann C. Noble, has this to say:

*Since quality is a composite response to the sensory properties of the wine, based on our expectations which have been developed from our previous experiences with a wide range of wines and our own personal preferences, this judgement is an individual response. No two people integrate the individual attributes in the same way, much less have the same preferences.*

I think that statement is worth rereading.

All wine evaluation is about a search for quality. It's an attempt to negotiate the disputed territory between objective standards and personal preferences.

We don't judge our favourite jug red in the same category as we judge a great Californian cabernet any more than we'd judge a Jeep in terms of a Rolls Royce, 'though both may be recognised as quality products. They're aimed at different social occasions, different people and different prices! Our expectations have begun to define our concept of quality by setting up relevant categories of judgement. Cost may well be a factor here. Within such general categories, further expectations are set up by our own experience. Allowances may be made for brilliant intuition, but on the whole, the greater our range of experience – in wine, as in art or music or literature – the better our judgement, and the more authoritative our sense of quality is likely to be.

Anticipation plays a part in enjoyment and appreciation of all human activity from sex to fishing or listening to music. Anticipation *can* be misleading – as witnessed by the hordes of 'label-drinkers' – but, if properly developed, it can be a positive factor in determining quality. Indeed it is one of the arguments of this book that the anticipation of a wine – what its sight and smell say to us before we ever put it in our mouths – is a large measure of our joy in it.

Whatever you do, don't be browbeaten or intimidated by fancy labels or prices; write down your own definition of quality. One thing is certain – it will definitely change with your socio-economic ups and downs!

# SIGHT – COLOUR

We do not see with our eyes alone;
we need light so that our eyes may form
images of objects – and a brain to interpret
the meanings of the nerve impulses.

# COLOUR – ALL IMPORTANT

Near Melbourne Australia, lives a young man, totally blind since birth, who, after smelling and tasting a wine, is able to comment, 'Gee, that wine has a beautiful colour!' – and he's always right. Through experience, this highly skilled winelover has learnt that life and freshness in wine, regardless of age, will equate with a desirable colour.

Why then, in a reverse context, are perfectly sighted tasters unable to determine much about the 'nose' and taste of wine from its colour alone? Are we lazy, or untrained? A bit of both, and because we lack awareness in observation – and, wine colours. One might ask the question: 'Can't the average person make a valid judgement about food by sight alone? Can't we tell whether vegetables or meat are overcooked without even placing them in our mouth?'

Generally speaking, sight – and in particular the discrimination of colour – is possibly our least trained sense. Although researchers tell us that when colours are lined up side by side the normally sighted are able to make something like 300,000 relative judgements, in practice we use only a tiny fraction of this innate ability. If we have a random test, without the benefit of comparisons, even the most colour conscious can identify only about eight or nine hues. Our language reflects our limitations. The Eskimos are reputed to have over 40 words for snow, reflecting the extraordinary ability to discriminate within the dominant colour of their culture, whereas dwellers in more temperate regions are severely limited in their perception and language. Think of how many words you know for yellow? Why do we call a white wine white, when that is one colour that it is not! Colourless, green, yellow, gold, straw maybe, but not white.

Women tend to be more colour conscious than men – a consciousness that is perhaps due to early childhood training, particularly in relation to clothes. Men will go out and buy a brown or grey suit without much thought given to the exact shade; there is not much choice anyway. What men buy is a suit that looks and feels good. Women, on the other hand, will spend a lot of time and concentration searching for a desired shade and texture in the dress material, and then follow up with a search for perfectly matched shoes and accessories. Not surprisingly, this ability to discriminate gives women a head start when it comes to wine appraisal, particularly the important questions of colour and clarity.

## COLOUR BLINDNESS

Another male handicap is that in our society, about eight per cent of the male population is colour defective, colour 'blind', while less than one half of one per cent of females suffer from this genetic problem. There are 11 different forms of inherited defective colour vision, all varying in severity from total colour 'blindness' to forms so mild that the individual may be unaware of the defect.

There are three kinds of cone receptor (nerve endings) to the retina of the human eye. These receptors vary in their response to different coloured lights and are consequently called blue, green or red cones, depending on the colour of the light to which they are most sensitive. Any problem with these cones causes us to be colour defective. These cones absorb light energy and generate electric impulses that travel along the optic nerve to the brain. People with normal colour vision will match colours, and mixtures of colours, in a very similar way. Normal eyes can match a spectrum yellow by a suitable mixture of spectrum red and spectrum green. The colour defective require much more green, or red –

depending on the nature of their ailment – in the red/green mix to match the spectrum yellow. This is a fairly severe handicap when assessing red and ageing white table wines.

## PERCEPTION TRAINING

Perception is the complete process of receiving information through one of the senses, comparing this information with past experiences, identifying it, and evaluating it. Visual perception is a skill we learn while growing up; it does not appear immediately in a newborn infant.

I will repeatedly say in this text that the brain is selective in the information that it filters for storage and recall. As in the other aspects of appraisal (smell, touch, pain, taste) only those subjects that we concentrate on, and train ourselves in, will be stored away for future recall. Training in colour discrimination during everyday activities will improve our ability to discern colours, and their meaning, in wine. Just look out the window and see how many shades of green you can isolate. How many whites, reds and browns surround you? And what effect does light and shade have on colours as you see them on your way to and from work or from your office or kitchen window?

Make the training more scientifically controlled by experimenting at home with a few bottles of food colouring. Half fill four glasses with water, add a few drops of red colouring to one glass, double the number in the next glass. There will only be a slight difference in saturation. Keep adding drops until you obtain a deep red. Now add one drop, then another, of blue and note the changing tints. In the other glasses add yellow colouring in the same proportions, then add a drop of green. Intensify the colours and then ask a friend to bring you random glasses to test your powers of discrimination. Apart from a general enlargement of our aesthetic responses, the underlying premise of such training is a recognition of the importance of colour in wine evaluation.

## COLOUR CAN DAMN

On one occasion I attended a vintage port tasting, in Boston, with a group of experienced tasters, many professional, and was flabbergasted that, after 13 wines, not *one* of the group mentioned the colour of *any* wine in their comments, even though the best wine in each 'flight' was obvious from its colour alone. The 'in mouth' evaluation of these wines did nothing but confirm what was apparent from the visual appearance.

An indication of the importance of colour and appearance in wine is the importance placed on these two factors in wine competitions. They are always an explicit component of the score, generally about 15-20 per cent, (I think it should be 40 per cent), thus an extra half point scored in this section of the judging can make the different between earning a gold or silver award. But, on the other hand, a competition wine can be rejected by the judges on colour *or* clarity alone, without any further appraisal. Colour can be this damning!

Most wines are scored on a 'modified' Davis system (there are several of these) one of which provides:

Colour and appearance – maximum four points.

Aroma and bouquet – maximum four points.

Volatile and total acidity – maximum four points.

Sweetness and body – one point each.

Flavour, bitterness, general quality – two points each – making a total of 20 points.

The normal allocation of points for awards is: Gold 18.5-20, Silver 17.0-18.4, Bronze 15.5-16.9.

Even for the layman, colour is a crucial part of the total aesthetic appreciation of wine. I wish I could stand on the roof of every city hall in the world and shout aloud, 'wine is all about colour and smell'. To the sceptic, intent on drinking as much as possible, who declares that it is all about taste, I would point out that, technically, the oral cavity (don't talk about the tongue) can register only four taste sensations – sugar, sour, salt and bitter (as explained in following chapters). What we normally call 'taste' is very largely smell and touch which, when combined with taste, makes up the overall flavour impression.

Music is a good analogy of discrimination. The difference between a good and a brilliant performance is the ability of the musician to interpret the nuances of the composer's finer points. Equally, the skill of the winetaster can be measured by his or her ability to interpret the nuances of colour and appearance. Colour and appearance are the first important aspects of wine appraisal – the starting point for 'harmony' in wine, when colour, smell and flavour are perfectly integrated.

## ORIGINS OF COLOUR IN WINE

Colour in wine comes mainly from two sources – grape skins and oxidation. The net contribution from these sources is dominated by the pH and sulphur dioxide levels in the must and wine.

The juice colour of most winemaking grapes is similar to lemon juice – only a few varieties have pink or red juice. The colour and character of all red wines comes from the skins, with some flavour contributions from the seeds and stalks. The red pigments of wine grapes are called anthocyanin and these, with related phenolic compounds, are derived by extraction during fermentation. These compounds are what differentiate, in the senses of sight, smell, touch and taste, red wine from white wine. The style and character of a particular wine are largely determined by the quantity and condition of the phenolic compounds, including anthocyanins. As much as five g/liter of total phenolics may be present in a young, red wine, but the anthocyanin level will rarely reach one g/liter. All anthocyanins are derivatives of the basic flavylium cation structure and it is the flavylium cation that gives anthocyanins their colour. At a pH of 3.4-3.6 20-25 per cent of the anthocyanins in wine are the coloured flavylium cation form, while only 10 per cent exist in the cationic form at a pH of 4.0. Hence, the ability to measure quality by colour alone.

The second source of colour is oxidation, which is the enzyme mediated action of oxygen substrates, primarily phenols, in the fruit or juice. Oxidation is the brown discolouration that appears when we cut an apple or pear (and so many other fruits and vegetables). Grape juice and wine suffer the same browning when exposed to uncontrolled oxygen. Other than in small amounts, oxidation is, generally, a fault in wine. Sherries and some table wines are aged in oak barrels under conditions of controlled oxidation; this is, in most cases, a desirable situation. Although grape skins and oxidation are the two primary sources of wine colour, there can be other factors affecting colour that the evaluator should know about. Briefly, these are:

*The grape variety.* Some grape varieties have higher concentrations of pigment in their skin. We expect a cabernet sauvignon, zinfandel or syrah to be a deeper colour, 'thicker', than pinot noir or gamay grapes.

*The maturity of fruit.* Colour builds up as the fruit approaches optimum ripeness – beyond that point colour starts to deteriorate as the skins break down.

*Climatic zones.* The chemical balance of cool climate fruit is different from the same variety grown in a warm region. Grape skin thickness can vary from six to fifteen per cent of total grape weight. Thicker skins are consistent with cooler climates thus providing more phenolics (pigments and tannins) during fermentation.

*Soils.* Soils rich in iron produce a more scarlet colour, as do warm, dry summers.

*Fermentation techniques.* It is during the primary fermentation – when the grape sugars are converted into alcohol (ethanol) and $CO_2$ – that the wine style will first be determined. The length of time the winemaker leaves the red/black skins in contact with the fermenting juice really dictates the style and colour. Higher temperature fermentations, around 80-90°F (25°-28°C), will be responsible for quicker extraction of phenolics.

*Daily 'pumping over'.* Pumping the juice over the skins is a major contributor to colour extraction, otherwise the skins, called the cap, sit on top of the juice and no extraction takes place.

*The reaction of anthocyanins and tannins.* While anthocyanins are the most important pigments in young red wines, they are progressively incorporated into polymeric tannin type materials with ageing, and the tannin itself becomes a pigment with a brick red colour that typifies an aged red wine.

*Sulphur dioxide.* Recent work by Dr T.C. Somers at the Australian Wine Research Institute suggests that wine colour (and consequently wine quality) is dominated by pH and sulphur dioxide ($SO_2$) levels. While the technicalities of these factors is beyond the scope of this book, I may summarise them by saying that it is desirable for table wines to contain a low pH, and therefore high acid levels, while at the same time having acceptably low levels of $SO_2$. High pH is responsible for less vibrant colour as the chemical form of the pigment moves to violet or colourless form. As pH increases so hydrogen ions dissociate to produce anions – these are more prone to oxidation thereby increasing the need for $SO_2$, the primary anti-microbial agent in wine-making.

This starts a 'dog chasing its tail' reaction as explained in the chapters on smell and taste. However, I will add at this stage that there are moves afoot in California, Germany and Australia to make some table wines without $SO_2$. The articulate Zelma Long, at California's Simi winery, relates that without $SO_2$ being added before fermentation, a natural 'fining' takes place during fermentation. A class of phenolics in white grape juice called catechins, which like to turn brown or oxidise – as mentioned above with the cut apple or pear – do exactly that. These brown phenolics combine with dead yeast cells in the juice and settle out of the wine. The long term benefit is a wine that is naturally colour stable and resistant to oxidation.

*Oak barrels*. Barrel ageing of grape varieties that attain optimum ripeness, e.g. chardonnay, chenin, sauvignon, semillon, allow for 'fuller' yellow-gold colour. This comes from the juice contact with the ripe skins (more yellow, less green) from six to 48 hours contact before fermentation, slight extraction from the barrel staves during maturation/evolution, plus limited amounts of oxygen during the process. These all contribute to a deeper saturation of colour.

*Ageing/evolution*. Like people, all wines should change with age. (These are not necessarily positive changes!) Red wines get progressively less intense, passing from red through ruby, brick red, to mahogany, then tawny and finally amber brown. At this stage, the colour of the wine is solely the colour of the tannins, the anthocyanins are long gone. White wines, on the other hand, through oxidation grow darker with age moving from straw to golden shades, then brown, and finally to a maple syrup colour.

## THEORY OF JUDGING COLOUR AND APPEARANCE

Any colour can be described by making use of three attributes, hue, saturation and brightness. In the textile, dyestuffs or paint industries, for example, these attributes are:

### HUE

This is the red, yellow, green and blue (or intermediate between adjacant pairs of these) tints that comprise our wine colour. Black, white and neutral grey have no hue. In a 'blind tasting – or one held under red lights – only a small percentage (20-30 per cent) of tasters can tell the difference between red and white wine; this is simply a lack of training. So, when we can see wine in good light, we should pay particular attention to the various aspects of sight since they are not only part of the aesthetic enjoyment of wine, but a valuable guide to its quality. Colometric measurements at the Australian Wine Research Institute, with both local and French wines, support the proposal that young red wines of superior quality can be determined by colour measurement alone. The colour levels of the wines measured varied from 6-25 per cent.

### SATURATION

Vividness of hue, depth of colour. Scarlet is a saturated colour, pink is a desaturated colour. Remember when we were adding more food colouring to the glass of water — we were saturating the hue. In red wines this saturation comes from optimally ripe fruit – unripe fruit will lack saturation of colour. Saturation is the degree of strength or intensity of colour in a wine. Red wines, for example, can vary from a light rose to a deep purple, depending on style, the term 'red being almost as loose as 'white'. Density of colour can be related to 'body' in a wine, full bodied being thicker, darker than 'light bodied' wines. The winemaker's use of sulphur dioxide is relevant here. While a certain amount of $SO_2$ may be a good thing to prevent oxidation and bacterial spoilage, excessive use of it (which seems to be a common practice in white wines from many French and German makers) will bleach wine colour. It is not uncommon to observe a wine six to ten years old that has absolutely no natural colour development. White wines that do not show saturation of colour from four to five years of age will, more likely, give off offensive odours (mainly $SO_2$) during the olfactory appraisal.

## BRIGHTNESS OR LUMINOSITY

Of colour's three attributes, brightness is the most difficult to define. Technically, brightness applies to an object that emits or reflects light. Brighhtness is an important part of clarity (see below), yet as an aspect of sight, especially in wine, it goes further. Relevant terms are brilliant, sparkling (non bubbly), as distinct from cloudy, dull, opaque. One might think of it as the difference between glass (clear) and diamonds (sparkling). All good wines – even an aged red – should be bright. Brightness is a visual sign of healthiness in wine; a dull or flat appearance suggests decrepitude or high pH.

## CLARITY

The other important aspect of appearance is clarity. At several stages during processing, from the crushing of the grapes to pressing the fermented skins, the must (fermented juice) looks like thick soup – minestrone, French onion or pea soup, depending on your individual preference. By a series of cleaning up processes – fining with eggs, colloidial clay or dried bull's blood, filtration through asbestos pads, diatomaceous earth or sterile pads, or just through natural settlement and racking – the finished wine is bottled free of any impurities. Even in the clearest juice, there lie lurking bacterial microbes waiting for a particular set of circumstances to spoil the wine. The spoilage agents may have been in the new bottles, corks, filtering equipment or the filtered wine.

## TURBIDITY

In simple terms, turbidity is the opposite of clarity. It is particulate matter, the material that causes haze or turbidity and protects microbes from the killing action of disinfectants, that gives us bacterial spoilage. For this reason the winemaker eliminates every possibility of turbidity. The American public health authority defines turbidity as 'an expression of the optical property that causes light to be scattered and absorbed rather than transmitted in straight lines through the sample'. This scattering and absorption is caused by the interation of light with particles suspended into the samples. Turbidity can be caused by clay, microbes, organic matter, and other fine, insoluble particles. Turbid samples have a hazy or cloudy appearance.

Although there are hundreds of millions of bottles of wine processed each year, faults are rare. Many winelovers never see a bad bottle of wine. But just to alert you to the possibility, here's how to go about checking your wine for clarity. Many of the visual defects will be accompanied by an unpleasant 'nose'. First, look at the surface of the wine as it can reveal much information. Well made wines, from small or large wineries, are normally sparkling bright or even brilliant in appearance. Any sign of haze, smokiness, milkiness or oily surface should be treated with suspicion. Cloudy or dull wines are usually spoiled with bacterial infection, yeast proteins, pectins or maybe metal salts. With today's technology, most wines, particularly white table wines, are stabilised before bottling. This is a process designed to eliminate, by chilling and filtering, harmless tartrates and to create the clarity and brilliance we expect from good wines.

The demand for clarity is not incompatible with the desirable sediment we find in good reds and some ports. Just as red wines take their colour and tannins from the grape skins, both the colour pigments and tannins can precipitate in the bottle and become sediment in table wines and vintage ports. This sediment, which starts to precipitate after about three years, is deposited by tawny and ruby ports in the barrel prior to bottling. The tartrate crystals, that are normally removed by stabilisation in white wines, form on the inside of the barrels and become known as wine 'stones' or 'diamonds'. Frankly, I find it encouraging to see the phenolic sediment adhering to the side of a red wine bottle, this being an indication that the wine has not been over processed and that some of the real natural grape elements are still intact.

## VISUALLY APPARENT FAULTS

Having said that, for the purpose of pointing out that all sediment and suspended material is not indicative of poor quality, most other visual impairments are to be treated with the utmost caution. It is not the scope of this work to examine in detail the numerous origins of these faults – but some of the main ones are listed here:

Bacterial spoilage is the principal cause of cloudy looking wines, and you can accept my word that such wines will not be good for anything – and that includes marinating meat!

Active lactic acid bacteria in sweet wines will leave a silky sheen or haze when the glass is swirled and the wine may develop an oily opalescence. It is almost impossible to remove all yeast cells after fermentation (although we are coming closer to that technology) and if there is sugar in the final product, the cells can spring to life again and begin secondary fermentation.

A source of smokiness in whites and dullness in reds can be malolactic fermentation, one of winemaking's love-hate syndromes. In cool climate, high acid wines, it is desirable to convert the malic acid of the grape to the softer lactic acid, thereby reducing total acidity. But, in warm growing regions where a goodly portion of total acidity is respired from the fruit before picking, this secondary fermentation that further reduces acidity, is not really welcome. It takes away 'life' from the wine, leaving it 'flat' and without appeal. Should this take place in the bottle rather than beforehand, several problems can arise.

The first, a build up of carbon dioxide in the bottle will create a similar effect to 'sparkling burgundy' when poured; secondly, the wine will be cloudy. Wines with this, not unusual, fault may eventually settle to a clear state over a period of three or more years without any deterioration of quality.

## HEALTHY VISUAL SIGNS

Bubbles are generally a healthy sign; they are the great delight of sparkling wines – 'beaded bubbles winking at the brim' as Keats noted. The bubbles in wine are carbon dioxide gas, created in sparkling wine at considerable expense. In still white wines bubbles are what the Germans call 'spritzig' and the French 'petillant' and are a sure sign that the wine has been carefully handled (but no guarantee of quality) at bottling time. To avoid the traumas of oxidation, new bottles are purged of oxygen by inert gas prior to filling and the wine in the storage tanks is held under a blanket of gas, once again, to keep it free of the enemy oxygen. As white wines are bottled very cold, some of this gas is taken into solution and appears in the bottom of the glass when poured.

Legs or tears are another phenomenon associated with the visual aspects of wine. There is probably more nonsense written and spoken about 'legs' than any other facet of appraisal; maybe because it's the first of the fallacies that the tyro learns about. The most common myth is that these tears running down the sides of the glass indicate high alcohol wines. False! It's only necessary to take a nip of brandy (40 per cent by volume alcohol), swirl it in your glass and you'll notice that the legs are almost non existent. Yet take an ounce or two of a sweet white table wine at 10 per cent by volume of alcohol, swirl that in your glass and you have real legs. The answer comes in two parts – first is the difference in surface tension between water and alcohol, the second is the viscosity of the wines, the differential evaporation of alcohol, sugar and glycerols combining with the wine. All in all, legs and tears are best kept out of wine talk; most wine people find it a subject of little interest.

## OBSERVING COLOUR – LIGHTING

To achieve maximum results in evaluating wine colour we need the best possible lighting available. Few people have it – most will never use it because, as yet, there is no such thing as standard lighting for wine assessment. Lighting specialists know much about illumination; wine people know little or nothing of the light needed for evaluation. We talk about 'daylight' as though it was a standard commodity – nothing could be further from the truth! Daylight is different in the morning, noon and afternoon; clear blue skies vary dramatically in light value to overcast skies; lighting in the northern hemisphere is much softer than the world below the equator. Lighting studies indicate that colourists, artists, and the like, prefer the light from a natural, moderately overcast north sky.

The production of colour requires three things: a source of light, an object that it illuminates, and the eye and the brain to perceive it. This is where we run into the first problem – subjectivity – colour exists only in the mind of the viewer. The relative insensitivity of the eye limits the visible part of the spectrum to a very narrow band of wavelengths, between 380 and 750 nanometers – a nanometer being a unit of wavelenght; one nm = 1/1 000 000 mm, there are 25 mm to one inch.

At the bottom end of the scale we start with violet (380-440 nm), blue (440-490), green (480-560), yellow (560-590), orange (590-630) and red (630-700). Hues are not really clearcut as they blend into each other, as blue-greens, green-yellows all along the spectrum. Purple is a mixture of red and blue from opposite ends of the spectrum. At wavelengths below 390 nanometers we have ultraviolet light and X-rays, while above the red hue there is infra-red and radio waves.

### METAMERISM

If the light source changes, the stimulus to the brain differs and we can expect the perceived colour to differ also. So we have a situation where our suit buyer selects a brown suit in a store with warm tungsten lights only to find that in daylight the suit will be another colour! This phenomenon is known as metamerism, and has an important role in wine colour assessment. Indeed, it is the cardinal reason that wine judging should have a standard light source. By definition metamerism is 'a change in observed colour depending on the nature of the illuminating light'.

If we take three colours of different pigments, A, B and C, that, for the normal sighted, will match under one light source, we find that, say, under daylight conditions, colours A and B will match and C will be the odd colour. But when we view the same colours under cool white fluorescent, B and C will match and A will be the odd one. Yet, if the same three colours are viewed under incandescent lighting, none of the three will match!

The amazing phenomenon of metamerism, combined with the known facts that the perception of colour varies from one person to another, and that we don't have an accepted standard light source for wine appraisal, leads us to all sorts of conjecture. While the one constant attribute of wine colour is the wine itself, the other two elements of colour perception – the source of illumination and the perceiver – are changing with each appraisal.

Nowhere has this been more evident than in the round of Australian wine competitions which produce lottery-like results annually. (Many authorities tell me that Californian competitions produce similar variations.) Australia has, by far, the most frequent and competitive wine contests and for the 'down-under' winemaker, success in these contests is money in the bank. Two similar competitions for young red wines are held back to back in the cities of Brisbane and Melbourne. Wines from the same vintage batch are entered simultaneously in each contest. The Melbourne contest attracts between 150-200 entries for the young red wine event alone, and the overall Melbourne competition draws something like 2000 entries. Yet, although two different companies here have won one of the two competitions for three consecutive years, no one has ever won both with the same wine, submitted to the same specifications and judged within two weeks!

## VARIATION IN LIGHT SOURCE

How can we explain this anomaly? Certainly the human element is one variable; different judging panels operate in each city. But most of the judges are extremely competent winemakers (although I don't know that any of them has been colour tested!). However, the real variable – one that is never mentioned – is the lighting; there is no standard light source for wine contests. (In addition, there is climatic variation which we will deal with in the chapter on smell. Over 1000 miles further north, Brisbane is considerably warmer than Melbourne, providing superior conditions for olfactory evaluation.)

Just as wine components have many srange forms of measurement (percentage by volume or percentage proof alcohol, degrees brix or baume for sugar, grams per litre for sugar, cyanide etc), lighting's measurement is temperature Kelvin. The vast different in the various light sources is reflected below:

| | |
|---|---|
| Kerosene Lantern Wick | 2000K |
| Incandescent Light | 2850K |
| Cool White Fluorescent | 5000K |
| Daylight Macbeth | 7500K |

The three important factors here are:

(a) What wavelengths of the spectrum does each include?

(b) How do the light sources compare with each other?

(c) In what areas of the colour spectrum are they the same?

This is where disaster strikes anyone making colour judgements of wine.

As there is no constant standard natural daylight, the world authority on illumination, the French-based Commission International de l'Eclairage (CIE), has determined a standard which is shown as the continuous heavy black line; Xenon arc, which is shown as the small dotted line, follows the CIE recommendation rather closely, but what is sold as daylight fluorescent, shown by the broken line, falls apart in our areas of vital concern, more particularly in the red wine zone, and to a lesser extent in the green-yellow area.

The Macbeth Company has been working on this problem for more than 70 years to provide a standard, and the best possible duplication of natural daylight for artists, colourists and others who work in the field of critical colour matching. Over this long period, they've learnt that no fluorescent lamp has yet been made that can provide this lighting. Macbeth says that the only commercially feasible way to simulate light or daylight quality is with filtered tungsten lamps ref. ASTM Standard D 0 1729 - 69 (74).

And, if you want a really bad light source for wine evaluation, the traditional candle is about as bad as you can get! (It may be OK for wine clarity but not for colour.)

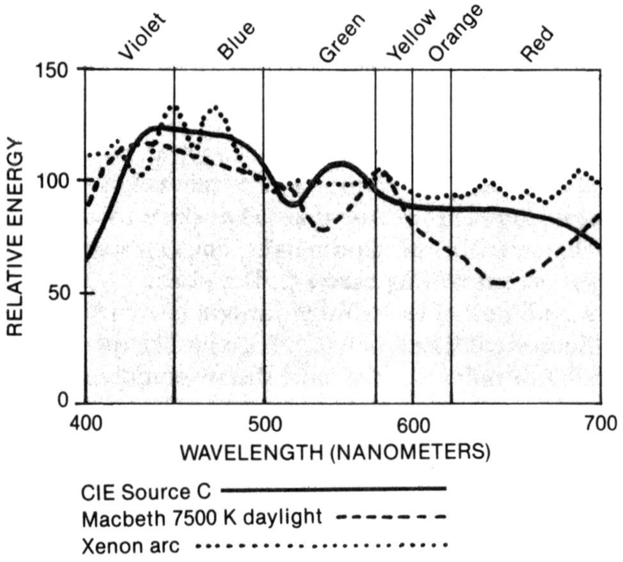


The spectral power distributions for some standard light sources used in describing colour (Wyszecki 1967, 1970).

I think these graphic examples explain the need for a standard light source, but I'm not the authority to do that. All I can do is warn of the obvious deficiency of human perception, something that is common to all nationalities. About this, we can do nothing. But, the subject of standardised lighting which will help minimise this problem, is within our resources; let's have some action!

## WHAT IS DAYLIGHT?

Natural daylight is variable. Lighting studies indicate that colourists, artists, finishers, etc. prefer the light from a natural moderately overcast north sky. Colour analysis of this light is shown in Curve 'A'. Note all colours are present in the light and that there is a little more blue than in the others, which accounts for the bluish characteristics of the North Sky Daylight. Curve 'A' then represents the ideal with which light sources are compared to determine how well the artificial source can be substituted for the natural one.

Since 1915, Macbeth has offered artificial daylight sources for critical colour work. The colour analysis for Macbeth Daylight as provided in the Macbeth Spectralight unit is shown in curve 'B'. Critical colour matching . . . the name applied to initial formulation of colour compounds to match a given sample . . . requires lighting which is the best possible duplication of natural daylight. The only commerically feasible way to closely simulate light of this quality is with filtered tungsten lamps. (Ref. ASTM Standard D-1729-69(74). No fluorescent lamp has ever been devised which can do the job as well, because even the special, colour-balanced fluorescent lamps emit high energy peaks of certain colours. These peaks mislead your colour judgement because that judgement is rooted in the 'smooth curve' characteristics of natural light. You can see these peaks very plainly in the accompanying curves C, D and E.

Note the smooth flow of the natural daylight curves (A) vs the abrupt changes of the fluorescent simulation (C). It's a bit like the effect you get when tuning your AM radio . . . the more distant stations vary slightly in their signal strenghts but when you hit the frequencies of local stations, your ears are blasted by the sudden high energy peaks. So it is with your eyes: they're blasted by the sudden peaks of energy which are present in all fluorescent lighting.

The argument that critical colour matching should be done under fluorescent lamps simply because the finished object will someday be viewed under fluorescent lamps, has no basis in fact. There is no more validity to this reasoning than there is to the thought that raincoats should be manufactured in the rain because they will someday be worn in the rain.

For the least exacting work such as shading, grading, inspection, etc, Macbeth offers the low cost Examolite® Fixture. This type of illumination is a blend of specially engineered Examolite colour corrected fluorescent tubes and Examolite 'long life' incandescent bulbs. The curve of the Examolite blend is shown in Curve 'D' and represents the highest degree of colour corrected 'simulated' daylight available with a fluorescent source.

Curves E and F represent ordinary fluorescent and incandescent light. Both of these lights have colour rendering deficiencies.

## THE VISUAL EXAMINATION

Having carefully chosen the best available glassware (see chapter 7) and the best available lighting, we now need an area devoid of strong colours that could reflect

CURVE A – NATURAL DAYLIGHT Natural preferred North Sky Daylight at 7400 Kelvin. Note that it contains a good balance of energy throughout the entire range of the visible spectrum.

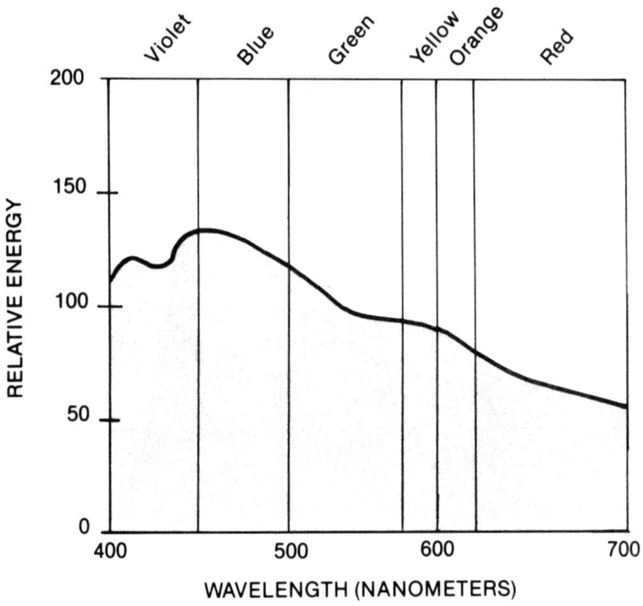


CURVE B – MACBETH FILTERED DAYLIGHT 'SPECTRALIGHT'®
Note how closely this curve reproduces that of natural North Sky Daylight across the entire visible spectrum.

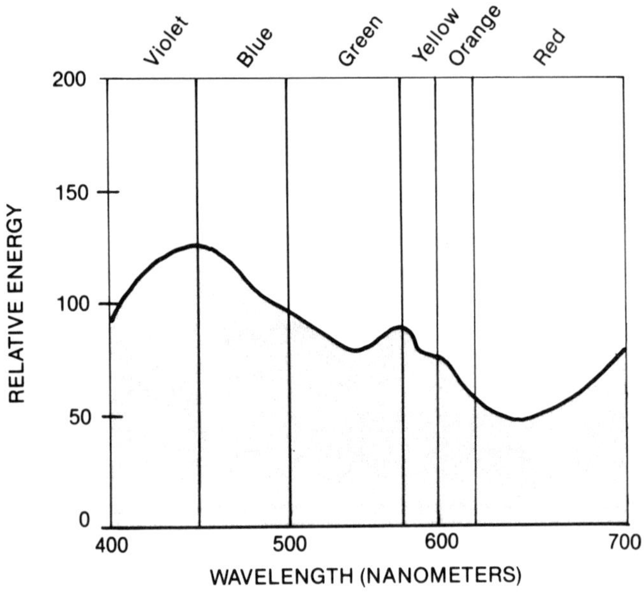

CURVE C – AVERAGE FLUORESCENT DAYLIGHT

Note the abrupt changes of the fluorescent simulation versus the smooth flow of the natural daylight curve.

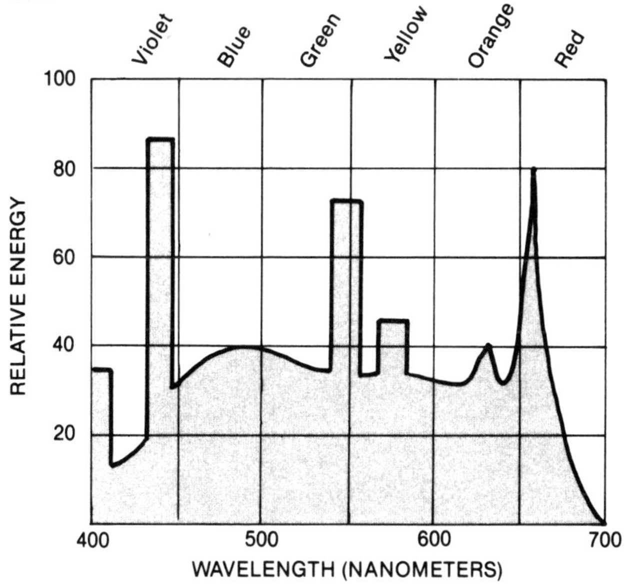


CURVE D – MACBETH BLENDED DAYLIGHT 'EXAMOLITE'®

This is the blend of special fluorescent tubes and incandescent bulbs. It is also a balanced energy source and is, again, a good simulation of natural daylight.

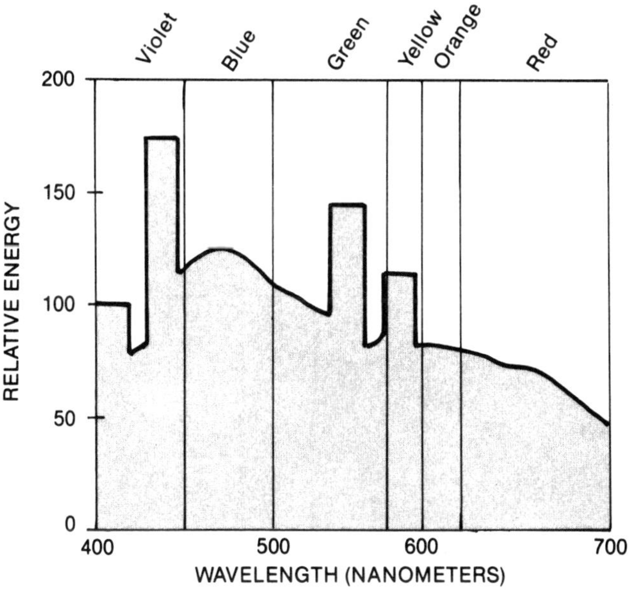

CURVE E – ORDINARY OR AVERAGE FLUORESCENT LIGHT

Note the deficiencies at each end of the spectrum which means that it is difficult to judge colour differences in these regions.

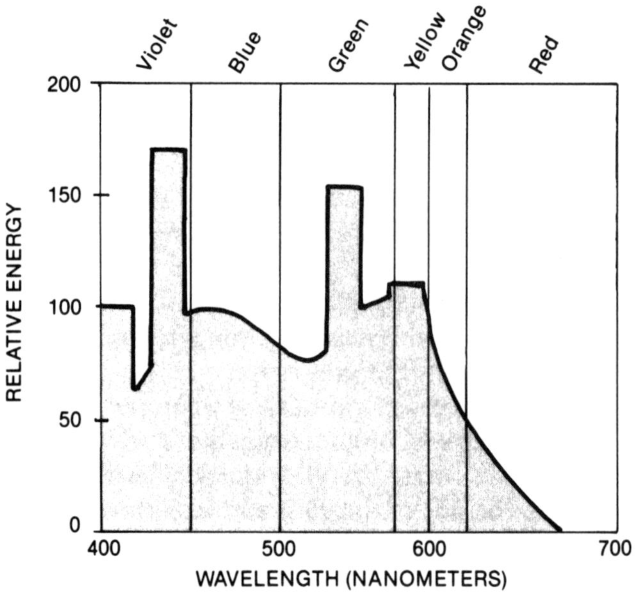


CURVE F – ORDINARY INCANDESCENT LIGHT

Here you will note the very high predominance in the red-yellow range of the spectrum as compared to the green-blue-violet range.

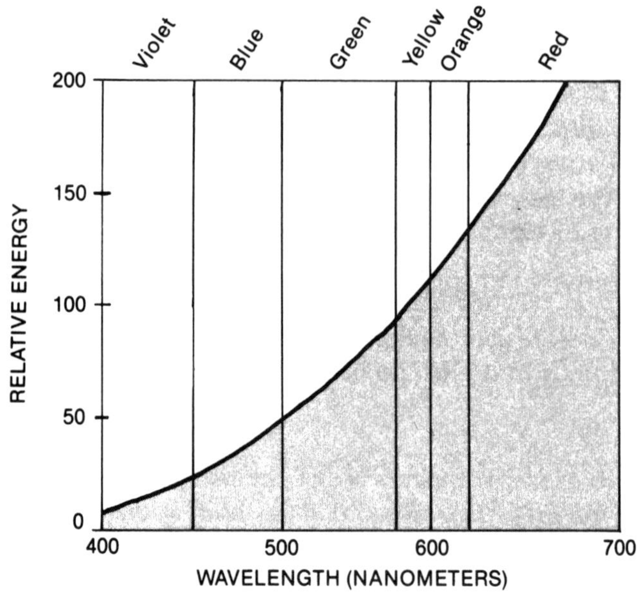

or conflict with the wine colours. White beneath and around the glass is the ideal, but in most instances it is sufficient to have a white table-cloth.

There are four positions from which wine colour can be examined:

1. I try to make evaluations as the wine is poured from the bottle – while it is between bottle and glass – looking at the wine as it's poured, or as it splashes in the glass; not easy, it requires a lot of concentration. Why not try this next time you see wine poured; a good background of white or light grey helps.
2. The most common everyday appraisal is when the glass of wine sits on the table and is viewed obliquely against a white background.
3. For critical analysis, rotate the glass quickly, swirling the wine so that it climbs up the side of the glass and look through the swirling wine; this will reveal any giveaway brown signs of premature ageing. (At the same time the swirling wine coats the total surface of the glass readying it for the olfacctory appraisal.)
4. Tilt the glass away from you so that a tongue of wine reaches the very rim of the glass. For red wine appraisal, I use a champagne flute. A flute allows for a long tongue and this is what must be examined. Here the heart and soul of wine colour is exposed.

## PURITY

First, look for the purity of colour – has a young red or white wine any of the spoilt factors that were discussed on page 23. Then check to see that there is no 'watery' rim around the edges, or on the tip of the tongue. Quality red wines with cellaring potential will have pure colour right to the meniscus – the very tip of the tongue and along the sides. Young white wines should be free of any signs of oxidation.

## SATURATION

Saturation of colour is our next concern as this will indicate the body or viscosity of the wine. If in doubt, go back and check page 21.

## APPEARANCE

Now, let us look at the appearance of the wine, starting with the surface, followed by the brightness. Record your observations on a score sheet, preferably the one recommended on page 35; which will ensure that you don't skip any of the fundamentals. Proceed with a preliminary olfactory and then a quick 'in mouth' appraisal, solely for the purpose of confirming your visual observations. Having smelled, felt and tasted the wine, go back to the visual aspects and check the relationship of colour-viscosity, colour-acidity, colour-nose, colour-flavour and colour-length of aftertaste. Look at the wine, think about each of these factors and next time you are speaking to a winemaker (or similar experienced person) discuss your findings. This is all a learned response requiring much application, lots of practice and concentration. Make sure that you spit out your taste samples, otherwise all wine will eventually look and taste great!

A word of warning. There are many so-called 'experts' who will tell you that colour has no association with wine quality. I can only say that if you follow the above procedures, you will arrive at a different conclusion, one that the world's leading researchers have determined.

## RED TABLE WINES

Young red table wines should have brilliant tints of red/scarlet/purple, depending on the growing region, grape variety, fruit maturity and condition.

As red wines age, both table and fortified styles, they progressively pass through the colours of ruby, mahogany and tawny as the colour pigments precipitate. Amber-brown is an acceptable colour; brown is one to be treated with the utmost caution.

While colour must always remain subjective, anything that approaches 'dirty' brown – such as the oxidised apple – is very much a minus factor. Orange browns that could be considered visually pleasing are usually indicative of good condition. However, aged coffee or chocolate coloured wines are an acquired taste and one should not necessarily like a brown wine just because it is aged. Wines of superior quality will always carry colour to the very edge of the tongue', and it is my studied belief that this is the first sign of a top class product.

During the ageing of red wines, there is some precipitation of tannins, tartrates and pigments – this is no problem, in fact, this becomes the sediment in wines. Most people prefer to decant wine from this sediment before serving. (There is a minority who prefer to keep the sediment, and, after disposing of the wine, enjoy it with freshly dug truffles!)

Among the normal ageing deposits we are likely to find tartaric acid crystals (wine diamonds) resting on the bottom of the bottle or, sometimes swimming around in solution. These are quite normal in vintage ports, red and some white wines.

The term red covers almost every colour from scarlet purple to the palest tawny – and each tint tells its own story. Reading these colours requires practice and experirence – much experience – but as the average winelover confines his or her imbibing pleasures to a limited number of styles and regions, this knowledge, by application and concentration, can be quickly gained. (You get out what you put in!) It's a different story for the professional taster whose skills must cover all districts and styles.

## WHITE TABLE WINES

White table wines range across the yellow colours from pale straw/yellow (like lemon juice) to rich gold, depending mainly on fruit ripeness and age. In a young wine, deeper colours will indicate ripe fruit and, possibly, some skin contact which will be further enhanced to deep gold tones with age.

Cool area wines will often have a green tint. Perhaps this is chlorophyl – maybe unripe fruit. If the wine is overly acid, lacking in flavour (as opposed to sugar) you can bet this is due to unripe fruit.

Above all, young white wines must be clear and brilliant; brilliant as diamonds. There are no ifs and buts about this statement. The ageing process will lessen this to a glasslike brightness. Traditionally, many Italian and Spanish winemakers have kept their white wines in oak barrels for several years prior to bottling, thus acquiring, to the unaccustomed, strong and unpleasant oxidative characters. This flavour is acceptable, in fact, the very essence of sherry style wines where these acetaldehyde produced flavours and bouquets are sought after; yet many winelovers dislike similar tastes in table wines.

Long bottle maturation will eventually see white wines develop brown to amber/brown colours. People with long experirence tasting these wines may enjoy them – I do – although most of today's winelovers prefer the freshness of young or current vintage whites. This has brought a change in wine-making philosophies in Spain and Italy.

## FORTIFIED WINES

Fortified wines are those with added alcohol, the popular styles being sherry, port, vermouth, marsala and the incredible Australian liqueur muscats and tokays.

### SHERRY – FINO

Let's start with the Spanish styles of sherry, a wine that has styles ranging from extremely dry to very sweet, although each style is made from 'white' grapes; all start with juice colours similar to lemon juice. The popular dry manzanilla and fino styles are bottled early after limited barrel and flor yeast contact, then consumed as young wines minus any oxidative colouring. They could best be described as pale fresh straw colour. Fino, in fact, means fine.

### SHERRY – AMONTILLADO

Amontillado is fino that has been kept in barrels for some years allowing it to become slowly oxidised and develop fuller viscosity and flavour through evaporation. This process brings about a golden, pale tan (old gold) colour and in my opinion adds considerable complexity to the style.

### SHERRY – CREAM

The sweeter, British cream styles are handled quite differently. Very ripe bunches of grapes are laid on mats in the hot sun to dehydrate, then after fermentation the highly sugar concentrate is left for years in barrel to darken and thicken; they are extremely luscious.

### PORT

On the other hand, the port styles of vintage, ruby and tawny, are made from red/black grapes – the style name is indicated by the colour. All ports start out almost crimson in colour when placed in barrels for maturation. Between one and two years the vintage ports are placed in impervious glass bottles so that 15-20 years later they still retain their youthful appearance. Ruby and tawny ports are left in barrels until sufficient colour pigments precipitate, giving them their respective colours of ruby or tawny. In the process they pick up some oxidative colour and flavours. The more time tawny ports are left in barrel the more colour pigments fall out and the wine finally becomes a true tawny with no red pigments at all. There comes a time in the evolution process when the sherries have picked up more oxidative colour and are darker than ports.

## APPEARANCE – ALL TABLE WINES – USEFUL DESCRIPTIONS

| POSITIVE | NEGATIVE |
|---|---|
| Clear | Dull |
| Bright | Cloudy |
| Star Bright | Precipitated |
| Brilliant | Gassy (Table Wines) |

Sparkling Wines – Bubble Size – Quantity, Rate, Duration.

## COLOUR – USEFUL DESCRIPTIONS

| WHITE | RED | SPARKLING WINES |
|---|---|---|
| Colourless | Pink | Same as White Table Wines |
| Very Light Straw | Rose | Blanc de Noir |
| Light Straw | Light or Purplish Red | Various Shades of Salmon |
| Straw/Green | Dark/Deep Red | 'Eye of the Partridge' |
| Fresh Straw | Tawny/Brick Red | Bronze – Coppery |
| Medium Yellow/Straw | | |
| Light Gold | | |
| Gold | | |
| Rich/Deep Gold | | |

## COLOUR SUMMARY

Do not rush into colour appraisal any more than you would bypass the visual aspects of food presentation.

Take a thorough and methodical approach, bearing in mind that the winemaker has taken at least two years to get a red wine in the bottle; please don't dismiss it in a few minutes.

Ensure that the lighting and ambience are the best available.

Use only well shaped sparkling clean glassware.

Carefully separate your appraisal of colour from appearance.

The two sources of colour are grapeskins and oxidation.

Tip the glass away from you so that a long 'tongue' exposes the body and soul of the wine. Practice reading the meniscus!

# SIGHT RECORD

These sheets have been designed to cater for *all* wine styles, in which case some material will be irrelevant to individual styles.

| PRIOR TO TASTING | |
|---|---|
| Appearance: | Brilliant, star-bright, bright, clear, dull, cloudy, precipitated. |
| Colour: | Colourless, very light/light/straw, straw green, light/medium/dark gold.<br>Blushing pink, rose, light/purplish/medium/dark/tawny/brick red. |
| Saturation: | Light, medium deep. |
| Bubbles: | Spritzig, size, quantity, rate, duration. |

## WINE EVALUATION RECORD

INTERNATIONAL WINE ACADEMY

Occasion L.A.D.V.

Place Washington Date

| | WINE RIESLING | PRICE | SIGHT 4 MAX | AROMA/ BOUQUET 6 MAX | IN MOUTH 6 MAX | AFTER-TASTE 3 MAX |
|---|---|---|---|---|---|---|
| 1 | FALL CREEK '85 | TX | 3.7 | | | |
| 2 | McGREGOR '84 | NY | 3.8 | | | |
| 3 | R. MONDAVI '85 | CA | 3.8 | | | |

| | | |
|---|---|---|
| 4 points | Excellent | Brilliant with outstanding characteristic colour |
| 3 points | Good | Bright with characteristic colour |
| 2 points | Average | Clear, without obvious faults |
| 1 point | Poor | Dull or slightly off-colour |
| 0 points | Objectionable | Cloudy and off-colour |

Please use fractions, ie ¼, ½ points, or decimal points.

It is an absolute *must* as you go through each of the exercises, that you practice your vocabulary – preferably with another person – for the given wine or solution. Use the words provided, or add any you think are easily understood and portable.

In this way you will quickly learn about each component; in addition you will build up a worthwhile vocabulary that can be understood anywhere. Please avoid the use of words with parochial meanings.

Words to describe wine *appearance* are:
Brilliant, star-bright, bright, clear, dull, cloudy, precipitated.

Words to describe *colour* are:
Colourless, very light straw, light straw green, light/medium/dark gold.
Blush, pink, rose, light/medium/purplish/dark/tawny/tile red.

# GLOSSARY OF COLOUR WORDS

ANTHOCYANINS: Anthocyanins are flavonoid, water soluble plant pigments which provide most the red, pink and blue colours in plants, fruits and flowers.
CLARITY: Clearness – opposite to turbid.
EXTRACTION: Extraction is what makes red wine different to white wine. Extraction during fermentation produces the colour pigments, tannins and aromatic substances.
FLAVONOID: A group of aromatic, oxygen-containing heterocyclic pigments widely distributed among higher plants. They constitute most of the yellow, red and blue colours in flowers and fruits. Anthocyanin is one of the four possible flavonoid sub-groups.
FLAVOUR: Flavour is a combination of odour, taste, temperature and texture.
MUST: Crushed grapes, or juice, until the end of fermentation when it becomes wine.
OPALESCENCE: A milky irridescence.
OXIDATION: Change in wine caused by exposure to air.
OXIDATION – REDUCTION REACTIONS: Oxidation and reduction always occur simultaneously with the transfer of electrons. The substances that gain and lose electrons are referred to respectively as the oxidising and reducing agents.
PHENOLICS: Phenolics are basically, the colour pigments (anthocyanins) and tannins which provide astringency.
PIGMENTS: Colouring matter.

# SMELL – OLFACTION

The sense of smell – the action of smelling.
From the Latin – olfacere, to smell.

If the international winelover has one common failing it is the enthusiastic desire to rush the wine into the mouth and start tasting. This act bypasses two of the more important senses – smell and sight.

Now, there's nothing wrong with rushing the wine into the mouth if one is simply in search of a drink. But, as we are discussing the sensory appraisal of wine, it's vitally important that we use some of our other senses before getting on with the business of drinking.

## THE CHEMISTRY OF SMELL

Researchers in many nations have long been interested in the nature of odorous substances, 'chemo-reception' as it is called technically, but effective study was made possible with the invention, only 30 years ago, of the gas chromatograph (GC). This is an instrument capable of separating complex mixtures of volatile substances (those which pass off easily in the form of a vapour, ie gaseous – or in the gas phase). Once an aroma can be separated into its various components, its chemistry can be studied.

The process of separation is not easy, mainly because so much of smell is elusive. Wine, for example, may give off several hundred volatile compounds that together may still represent only a few parts per million of weight. This volatile fraction, in turn, may contain only a few compounds that are odourous enough to make a contribution to the aroma and, more often than not, these are present in only trace amounts. It is said that only seven of 130 chemical elements are odorous; flourine, chlorine, bromine, iodine, oxygen (as ozone), phosphorus and arsenic. Most of what we perceive as smells come from volatile chemical compounds.

The modern gas chromatograph equipped with capillary columns, is a mechanised version of the human nose; it can separate 200-400 compounds from one particular wine or foodstuff. The chemist sniffs the effluent gases from the GC at frequent intervals and records observations. When strong odours are present they are described in simple terms such as 'green grass', 'oniony', 'rose-like'. These are recorded on tape and their position marked on the chart of the GC. Thus the peaks that correspond with strong odours are readily located and the compounds that make them are pinpointed for further study. If 10 compounds in the GC, for example, have been humanly identified with 'green grass', they are then further separated to see what chemical features they have in common.

While the GC effectively separates volatile substances it is unable to identify them. This task is performed by a mass spectrometer (MS) and it is fortunate that means were found to link these two instruments to form a powerful research tool – the GC-MS. Since every compound produces characteristic patterns of ions (electrically charged atoms) in its mass spectrum, that spectrum, for practical purposes, may be regarded as its finger-print and can be identified in the GC-MS.

### GREEN PEAS AND WINE

In the initial studies of the flavour of green peas, for example, the human nose acting in conjunction with the GC was used to recognise three compounds with intense odours. Subsequent studies over four years, during which time only a few micrograms of each material were able to be extracted, showed that the three were structurally related.

Here there was no problem of stereoisomers (two substances which may have the same basic structure but have different stereochemistry – the actual arrangement of atoms in space) but the chemical stability of the compounds prevented the collection of structural information by micro chemical transformations. Structures were predicted from their mass spectra and synthetic studies eventually gave the structures of the natural material. Their structure differs in only one grouping, which greatly influences the aroma of the compound.

From a winelover's point of view this has broken new ground, as we had not known what gave certain wines their particular fragrance. Compounds A and B with the isopropyl – and sec-butyl – groups have similar odours, akin to freshly opened green pea shells, but compound C with the isobutyl group is quite different. Its aroma is characteristic of green peppers or capsicums; similar aromas are found in the cabernets and merlot. These compounds are amongst the most odourous known and are present in fresh green peas in extremely small amounts – in the order of one part in 100 000 million! Recently these compounds have been shown to be present in varying small amounts in many other raw vegetables, including green beans, broad beans, lettuce, spinach, carrot and beetroot. They are now believed to occur commonly in minute amounts in many green plants.

## EARTHY

In beetroot, another highly odorous compound was detected. This substance, which has a strong 'earthy' odour was subsequently identified as geosmin, compound D, a known compound, which is the main aroma component of freshly turned earth. It is known to be produced by some classes of micro organisms in soils and in water catchments where it imparts an earthy quality to the water, and, no doubt, is responsible for the many wines given an 'earthy' classification.

In the future, it will be refreshing to attend wine tastings and hear references to the pyrazines and such terms as isopropyl, secbutyl, isobutyl, and geosmin in addition to the few compounds now recognised – diacetyl, $H_2S$ and $SO_2$, instead of the non specific adjectives that the 'in-set' use to bully their friends. And won't the earthy smell of geosmin be a nice piece of oneupmanship for the wine and food set?

For those with a penchant for the chemical structure of wine and food, this is how these chemicals are constructed.

# CHEMICAL COMPOUNDS

A

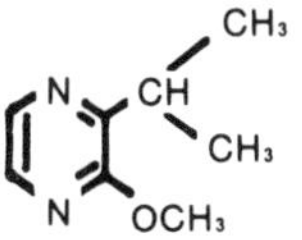

B

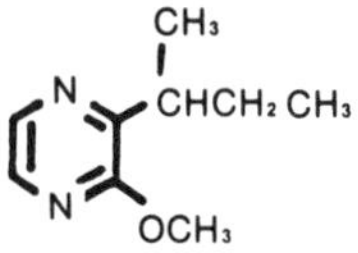

C

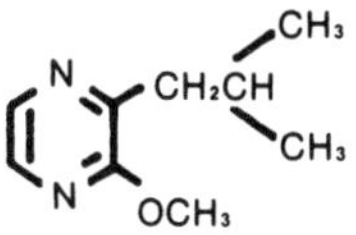

D

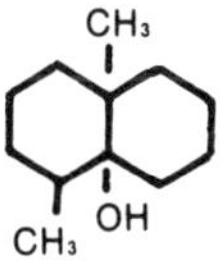

E

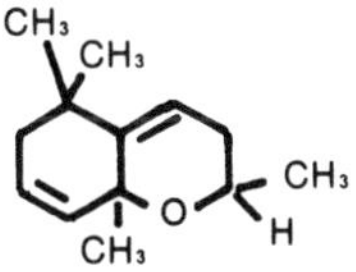

F

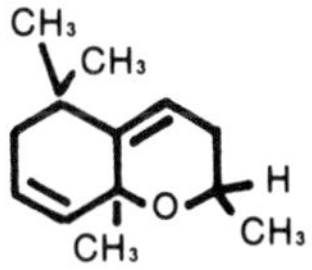

G

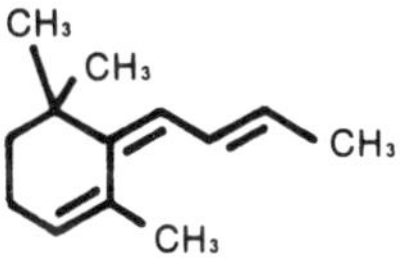

H

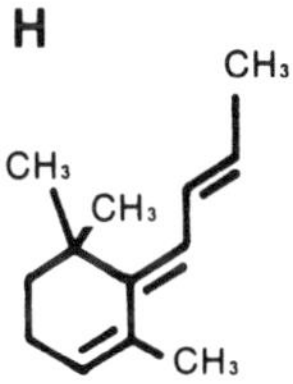

## FLORAL

In contrast, the aroma of the purple passionfruit[1] hasbeen found to be exceedingly complex and here again the use of the human detector (nose) led to the discovery of two novel classes of compounds. These were shown eventually to be structurally loosely related to beta-ionone, a principal perfume component of the flower of the brown boronia[2].

The compounds called the edulans of the megastigmatrienes, had strong rose like aromas. These, too, were available only in microgram quantitites, but unlike the green pea compounds they easily underwent chemical transformations on the microgram scale to yield compounds of known structures. This information led to the determination of the basic structures but in these cases the stereochemistry of the molecules was of importance.

The stereochemical structures of the edulans are compounds E and F and the megastigmatrienes are compounds G and H.

1. Passionfruit – a distinctive, popular seed fruit grown mainly in Australasia and Hawaii.
2. An Australian native flower.

## ADDITIONAL USES FOR ANALYSIS TECHNIQUES

The coupling of the gas chromatograph to the mass spectrometer was a giant step in the identification of components responsible for the aroma of wine and food flavours. The recent developments (circa 1970) of polymers (compounds of high molecular weight) capable of retaining the volatile organic compounds with the exclusion of water (or alcohol) have been an equally large step in the isolation and concentration of aroma substances. Prior to this development, classical techniques involving distillation, followed usually be solvent extraction and then concentration by evaporation of solvent were employed. Such a procedure frequently led to the destruction of sensitive but highly important aroma compounds.

The new collection techniques, when coupled to the instrumental power of the GS-MS, has allowed the research worker to undertake tasks previously considered impossible. Some examples include studies of the variation of flavour components between individual single fruits, the monitoring of changes taking place during fruit ripening, and the identification of differences in meat flavours produced by feeding animals on different diets or by the use of different slaughtering techniques.

Because of these successes, the techniques have been used to study such elusive problems as the chemicals responsible for metabolic disorders as evidenced by the excretion of novel metabolites.

Even though we are well down the road of chemical analysis, it is still not possible to identify wines made from individual grape varieties in the laboratory; we still have to trust the labels for a few years yet! It is also interesting to note that routine laboratory analysis cannot make any distinction between a great and an ordinary wine.

## CHEMISTRY

The most abundant volatiles of wine are aldehydes, alcohols and esters.

### ALDEHYDES

Briefly, aldehydes are derivatives of alcohol. When alcohols are oxidised they occupy an intermediate position between primary alcohols and acids which are formed on further oxidation. Vanillin in oak is an aldehyde. It is vanillin extracted from the barrel staves during barrel maturation, that provides the familiar vanilla smell that many winelovers recognise as oak in wine. Cut an apple in half, wrap one half in plastic wrap and cut the remaining half into segments. Smell the freshly cut segments, then allow them to go brown (oxidise) for 30 minutes or more. The fresh smell of apple will be replaced by the smell of aldehyde. Bring out your wrapped half, cut it into segments and smell the oxidised and fresh segments separately. Just for the record, more than 45 odorous compounds have been isolated that contribute to the aroma of an apple. And when we talk about the smell of an apple, what are we talking about? Cooking changes some of these odourous compounds — does an apple pie or apple juice really smell like a freshly cut apple?

Oxidation of wine can lead to the production of compounds such as aldehydes and acetic acid. As you will notice, the presence of aldehydes will greatly reduce the natural aromatic character of wine, or apples. (In small amounts, oxidation can also be a complexing factor; in any more than small amounts it is definitely a negative factor.)

## ALCOHOLS

Alcohols occur widely in nature as volatile or essential oils. By way of interest, raspberries and strawberries contain at least seven different alcohols; bananas seven (five are the same as strawberries); oranges about 15, and wine contains more than 15 alcohols.

## ESTERS

Esters are derived from acids by the exchange of the replacable hydrogen of the acid for an organic radical; esters or acetic acid are called acetates. Esters, aromatic compounds, are one of the main components monitored by the GC. The several types of esters found in brandy are responsible for the charaqcteristic aroma. The main esters in brandy are ethyl acetate (general fruity aroma), ethyl caprylate (pineapple), two phenyl ethanols (floral), ethyl caprylate, ethyl heptanoate, ethyl perargonate (all grape aromas). Aldehydes, also GC tested, are complexing agents that complex the esters. Fusel oils are higher alcohols that contribute to mouth feel. Smoothness is the fusel oil characteristic most familiar to the brandy sipper.

Important uses for low molecular weight esters such as ethyl acetate and butyl acetate are solvents for lacquers, paints and varnishes. Often these types of smells are associated with 'not good' wine. Synthetic, low molecular weight, esters are used commercially as the base for artificial food flavours. Some of these are: ethyl formate (artificial essense constituent in peach, raspberry and rum); ethyl acetate (in apple, pear, strawberry); amyl acetate (in banana and apple).

So, it can be seen that the volatile composition of a large number of fruits is similar, but their ratios and trace amounts of other compounds determine what the mixture smells like; whether it is apples, pears, strawberries or other fruits.

## TYPICAL AROMAS

With few exceptions the major portion of wine and grape aromas comes from the internal cells of the berry skin. In only a few varieties does the juice aroma dominate. I'm always fascinated when people talk about the 'typical' cabernet or chardonnay aroma. There is no such thing as typical, not even within one appellation.

Even in Bordeaux where cabernet is king, it is well documented that the cabernet aromas vary considerably from one vineyard to another. Their further different identification becomes a matter of psychology of smell, cultural background and the resource of language we have to describe it. Let's look at the detail of how our smell mechanism actually works.

## SMELL MECHANISM

Dogs are used for laboratory smell tests because of their legendary prowess in that field; two notable examples being their capacity to detect drugs in closed baggage, and from a mile away smell a bitch on heat – possibly the strongest smell in the dog's world, yet not one perceived by humans. We believe that the male moth has the same ability for a distance of 10 kilometres. These and other animals live mainly by smell, wheareas we mere mortals read labels and

and ask questions rather than use our senses. However, we can smell scatol at one part in four billion – or acetic acid at 40 000 times greater than we are able to taste it. Humans are little different in their smell physiology from dogs, rats and rabbits! (In fact, much of what we know about smell has been learnt from these animals.)

Our smell mechanism is divided into three main parts:

1. The receptors located in the olfactory epithelium at the top rear of the nose.
2. The neuro-transmitters (neurons) that carry the chemically charged message.
3. The central (olfactory) cortex which acts something like a switch-board distributing messages to various parts of the brain for response.

Our response to smell can influence learning, memory, sexual or emotional behaviour. As with taste and sight, each person has a different response to smell. Perfume, by way of example, does all sorts of things to people – why? Is it real, or imagined? And the many reactions to a burning smell from the kitchen are worth noting.

## EXTREME SENSITIVITY

Although the size of the olfactory receptor is about equal to a dime, that's not the real truth. The receptors (one on each side of the nose and brain), are made up of nearly 1000 finger like cilia, these have a surface or contact area of something like 3000 $mm^2$; this accounts for the extraordinary sensitivity of our sense of smell.

For smells to reach these receptors they must pass through ¾″ (18mm) of mucous membrane. Researchers believe that only 20 per cent of any available odour actually enters the nose, and of this amount only two per cent passes through the mucous membrane to make contact with the sensitive receptors. Unless we concentrate and make maximum use of this limited smell resource, our natural gift of smell sensitivity and power will be wasted. Those who train and apply this wonderful sense will find new pleasures and skills, not only in food and beverages but in many facets of their everyday life. Having a low smell threshold for several gases, I was once able to detect escaping gas and bring it to the authority's attention even though there were 300 other people in the same place who, apparently, neither could nor did smell the potential danger.

Fortunately, my work regularly takes me to Asia. Here I'm told that, like grapes, there are several hundred varieties of the cereal grain, rice. Rice buyers are able to rub a few grains in their closed hands and by smell alone determine the variety and country of origin. Wool buyers have the same ability with their product.

## SMELL – AND THE PAIN SENSE

In true wine terms, the act of smelling embraces another sense – the pain or irritation sense – and I continually notice, in many countries, that even keen wine judges completely ignore this sense during olfactory appraisal.

While we are smelling wine or food we can actually perceive physical irritation from, amongst other substances, alcohol and $SO_2$ through the free nerve endings in our nasal cavity.

Both alcohol and $SO_2$ are also 'touch' perceivable in the oral cavity; more about that in the next chapter. In the nasal cavity alcohol tends to irritate the bottom portion whereas sulphur penetrates further to irritate and dry the upper portion of the nose. $SO_2$ is strongly reminiscent of a safety match being lit. Asthma sufferers should acquaint themselves with the smell of $SO_2$ which is widely used as a food preservative and, wherever possible, avoid food or beverages containing it.

### TEMPERATURE

The most important tactile sense during the olfactory assessment is temperature. Even though it is comprehensively covered in a later chapter, it would be impossible to overstress its importance here. Wine that is too cold will have a 'dumb' nose or no nose at all.

## PHYSIOLOGY OF SMELL

When we enjoy flavoursome beverages of food we are largely experiencing their aroma – the combined effect of a number of odorous substances emanating from what is in our mouth. Most alcoholic beverages are consumed at temperatures between 40-70°F (5-20°C) and this low temperature inhibits many of the volatile fragrances. When taken into the mouth and warmed to body temperature by the saliva, the increase of some 20-30°F in temperature produces far more odorous substances in beverages than are available during the external nasal smelling from the glass.

These odorous substances diffuse by way of the back of the mouth up into the inner regions of the nose, where they encounter the smell receptor area. As mentioned earlier, this is composed of millions of highly specialised cells that are activated by odorous substances and transmit signals to the brain.

## LOCK AND KEY PRINCIPLE

There is a popular theory and one to which I subscribe, that odours and receptors work on a lock and key principle. If you have the right lock (receptor) then the key (odour) will open the door; the smell will register. Some molecules, carbon dioxide is an example, have a shape that will not stimulate the olfactory receptors and is, thus odourless. Yet in sparkling wines its touch effect is a pleasant sensation. Carbon monoxide (automobile exhaust fumes) is a killer gas due to it not being smell perceivable.

Odorous substances must be volatile, and soluble in water or fat so that they can pass through the mucous membrane and 'lock' onto the sensitive receptors. Another requirement for our 'key' is to have a molecular weight between 17 and 300 – above or below these optimum figures, the substances are less odorous.

### SMELL BLIND – ANOSMIC

I support a theory that we are all smell 'blind' or anosmic to particular smells – as opposed to not recognising previously unsmelt odours. Each individual has a different level of smell acuity and, I believe, perception to individual fragrances. This is, possibly, borne out by the wide range of men's and women's perfumes.

My own personal 'blind' spots are mint, nuts, oak and pepper which really limit my red wine repertoire. This selective smell blindness is different to

In this example various odours fit several binding sites in one receptor molecule.

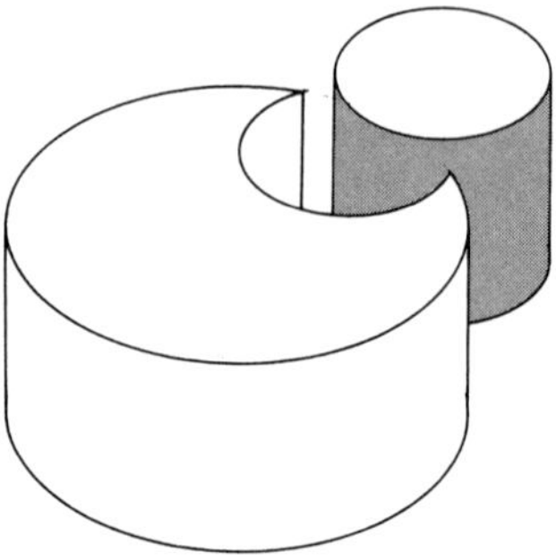

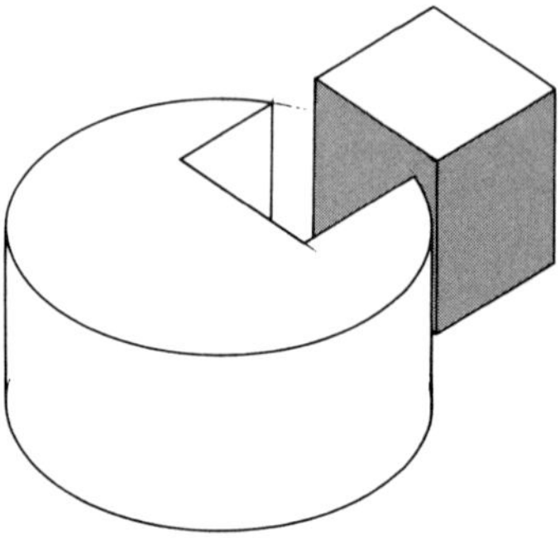

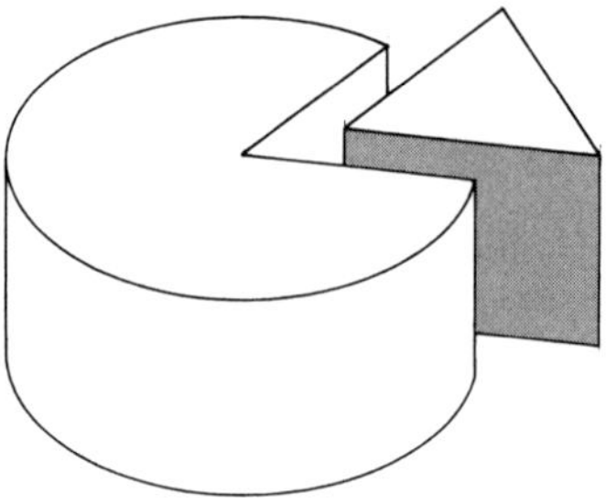

In this diagram each receptor binds only one odour.

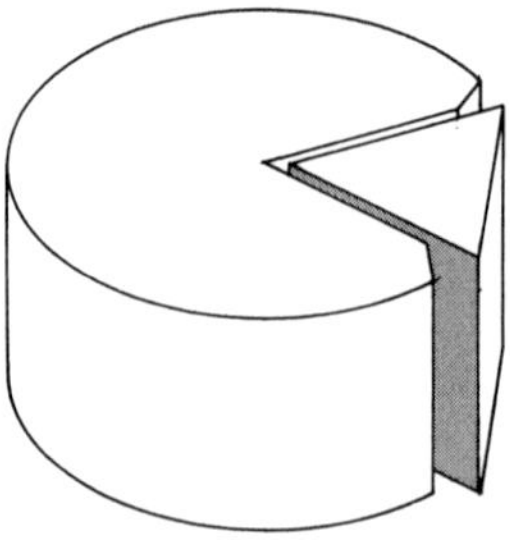

Tight binding.

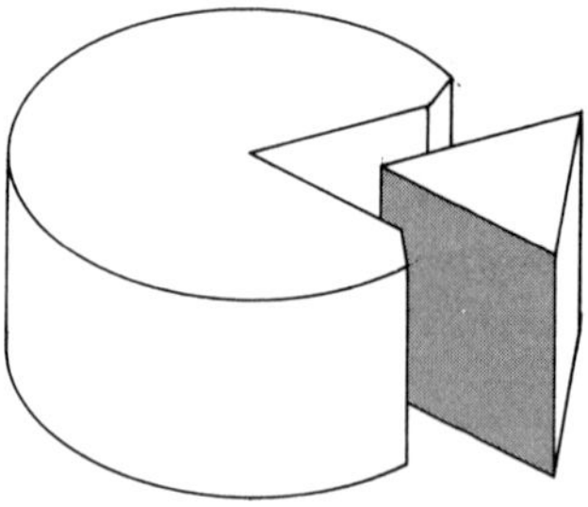

Loose binding. Rapid exit of odour molecules may lead to decreased response.

being anosmic – totally unable to smell – which is the fate of only about .01 per cent of the population. So it could be said that I have four keys missing from my house of locks.

### WOMEN MORE PERCEPTIVE

We did mention that women are more colour perceptive – the bad news for the male ego is that women are also more smell perceptive. This applies generally, but particularly during their menstrual period and the metabolic disarrangement of pregnancy. During this time some commonly acceptable smells are sufficiently repulsive to make them ill. It is not uncommon for women attending an education program spread over four weeks to report being more odour perceptive during their regular period.

## THE PHYSICAL APPRAISAL – SMELLING THE WINE

Before commencing any sniffing, swirl the glass so that wine covers the whole available surface area of the glass. If you're a sloppy swirler, tilt the glass so a tongue forms up to the rim and then roll the glass around, coating the inside surface area.

The more coated surface area, the greater the release of odourous compounds. Another useful method of coating the total surface of the glass, and also exciting the wine, is to place your hand or a plastiglas lid over the top of the glass and shake it rather vigorously, then put it to your nose before removing the cover. This is the most important method for critical examination.

Smelling and breathing are two separate functions, somewhat similar to walking and running. During normal breathing only a small amount of air contacts the smell receptor region, so a quick, deep, even forceful, sniff is desirable. Don't repeat this too quickly (no sooner than 40-50 seconds) as our smell organ fatigues easily. (Some people even find a forceful sniff counter productive and, of course, you don't want to hyperventilate!)

At the risk of labouring the point, it is important that you actually sniff the odours right up into the receptor area so that a worthwhile registration is made. At this time you will find that concentration is considerably aided by closing your eyes. Don't hold the glass under your nose and look at it as so many people do – sniff, and concentrate on nothing else. Should your smell power diminish to zero, try smelling a glass of water. This will give your smell mechanism some relief.

A large part of the brain's processing of sensory signals involves filtering and selection of stimuli and information, and particularly that relating to our own needs or environment. If we don't concentrate, we allow important information to be filtered out. After sniffing the wine, spend plenty of time thinking through your first impressions. Practice will tell that often only one sniff is ncessary – more than two or three sniffs are completely useless.

For a disciplined approach to smelling, make up your own check list: is the wine 'clean' (no dirty smells), fruity, sweet, varietal, woody, musty, oxidised, etc? Record the good or bad features of aroma, bouquet and touch on a scorecard or 'spider' as illustrated in the last chapter (page 123). Working hand in hand with your scorecard and the aroma wheel here's a quick check list as a basis for your olfactory appraisal:

| AROMA – from grape | IRRITATION | BOUQUET – from processing |
|---|---|---|
| Fruity | No response | Clean |
| Floral | Sulphur – perceivable | Fresh |
| Spicy | Alcohol – irritating | Dirty |
| Vegetative | | Yeasty |
| Earthy | | Perceivable sulphur – without irritation |

Now have a look at the intensity of smell.

| NEGATIVE – Too little | POSITIVE | NEGATIVE – Too much |
|---|---|---|
| Little or no smell | Balanced | Out of balance, i.e. too much wood, alcohol |
| Latent – Dormant | Varietal | |
| | Generic Style | |

Check your results on aroma wheel (page 55) working from the first tier, inside: fruity, vegetative, chemical, earthy, to the outside and more specific third tier: fruity, berry, strawberry, blackberry, raspberry, black currant.

## THE NOSE

The nose of the wine is made up from aroma, bouquet and (don't forget), irritation. Aroma is the fragrance provided by the fruit of the grape berry Bouquet covers the winemaking process such as yeast, sulphurs, oak treatment, maturation and other good or bad smells not directly related to the fruit. When commenting on the nose of wine be careful in articulating aroma – the fruit, bouquet – the processing element, and irritation – the feel.

Repeated sniffing causes confusion, olfactory tiredness and contributes nothing to smell registration. So make sure that you complete your smelling and checking in an orderly fashion. Smelling requires practice, just as marathon running does, and it's an area in which we can quickly lift our game with practice.

## IN THE BRAIN

Let's stop at this point and consider what's going on at the central computer room, the brain, as the smell stimuli are fed into the system. A whole mass of signals are demanding answers. Signals from the olfactory centre and other signals of pain or irritation (the touch sense) in the nasal passage. It is at this time we can estimate the alcohol or $SO_2$ content of wine, as above average levels will cause physical irritation to the nose and, maybe, the eyes.

Within a micro second the brain is asked to provide answers to these smell and touch queries, You, and only you, can help at this time, a time demanding intense concentration and orderly analysis of all the signals. Use your score card at this time, or some other recording sheet.

## SMELL SKILLS

Like a computer, the brain can only provide information that has been previously fed in. It must have, in our case, a 'smell bank' if it is to interpret what we smell. To accumulate a smell bank it's good to become smell inquisitive and try to file away every identifiable odour. Herbs and spices in your kitchen are good training as many of these have the same fragrances as wine. During any spare moments, have a friend give you random tests with anything that will help you develop your smell skills. Also try to identify the smells in the glasses and cups in your cupboards. If you use a towel for drying dishes it can be an amazing source of all types of kitchen odours, even the distinctive fragrances in the dishwashing detergent. But enough generalising – let's move on to the specifics.

There are four defined areas of olfaction to be carefully considered.

## EXTERNAL

The normally accepted method of smell appraisal is the straight-forward smell up into the nose from the glass. It is my strong belief that this external effort is really only a 'warm-up' for other more important appraisal methods.

## IN MOUTH

My main appraisal – the retro-olfactory – is made after the wine has been taken into the mouth (and then spat out, not consumed). This first gulp of wine is taken purely for olfactory, not taste or touch judgments. This retro-olfactory assessment is even more important if the wine is too cold for any worthwhile external judgment.

Nothing inhibits the natural fragrance of wine more than over chilling – a common fault. With very few exceptions, all professional judgments of wine are made at room temperature; this is a tough time for professional tasters of champagne (and not a very pleasant experience).

Having taken a gulp, the best way to maximise your efforts here is to close your mouth, roll the wine around, chew it like a steak. This chewing action also brings into play other sensory receptors, particularly in relation to texture. Then drop your chin moving the wine into the area behind the bottom teeth. With pursed lips, suck in some air over the wine just as though you were eating hot soup. (Whistle backwards!) The wine, warmed by the saliva, will release more molecules of volatile substances. These will rise through the rear nasal passage to the smell receptors. The more molecules released, the more positive the registration.

After the wine has been swallowed (expectorated for preference), close your mouth and breath out – or huff! This allows us to savour the wine. We smell by inhaling, savour by exhaling through the nose. This exhaling through the nose will also be a good indicator of which components are flavour and smell and which are taste. (Maybe, with very good wines, you can let a spoonful slip down your throat and this will certainly assist with critical flavour evaluations.)

## THE EMPTY GLASS

Anyone who's ever smelt an empty beer or whisky glass the morning after a party will know that smells have a habit of hanging around, particularly bad smells. This is equally true of our empty wine glass, which will have warmed somewhat following the disposal of the liquid, and have its total surface area coated, making available the maximum amount of smellable odour.

## PRIOR TO MOUTH

If we are alert and concentrating while the glass is being raised to the lips, almost immediately before the wine enters the mouth we will perceive the higher volatiles of the fruit flavour and bouquet. Watch very carefully for this

# SMELL PATHWAYS – EXTERNAL AND INTERNAL

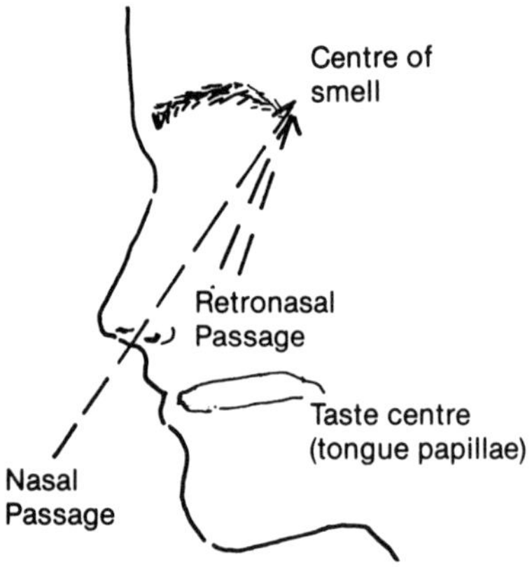


bonus smell opportunity. It appears as though we unconsciously take a breath before placing things in our mouth and at this time we inhale some of the more prominent odours.

Regardless of the method of appraisal, it is worth remembering that too little wine will not allow for a worthwhile appraisal, while too much wine will prevent the mouth from warming it sufficiently to release an increased amount of volatile substances.

WHAT DO WE ACTUALLY SMELL?

Here we run into three complex difficulties:

Physiological – What can we really smell? Do not be influenced by others.

Psychological – What do we anticipate or expect?

Linguistic – Do we have the language resources to convey our sensory perceptions?

In the first place we are smelling a coloured liquid and trying to related this to some common everyday commodity so that we can communicate our experience. It is easy to say that a flower smells like rose when we can see or feel a rose, but we are looking at a glass of wine, not a rose. (By way of interest, Singaporeans are the only culture able to consistently identify rose fragrances – Caucasians are very poor at recognising what one would think is an obvious smell.)

And what about the garlic eating cultures of the world? Is this smell so ingrained that they can't smell two of wine's major faults – mercaptans and $H_2S$, both smelling somewhat similar to garlic. Certainly New Zealanders living near the famous Rotorua thermal fields are immune to the wine destroying odour of hydrogen sulphide, a natural product of the local geysers.

And what expectations does a French person have when smelling an Argentine wine – or a Moslem breaking the faith in flavour of 'la dolca vita'? Can a top quality Argentine or Australian product cross these formidable cultural barriers and be accepted in their own right?

## COMMUNICATION

Having determined what we think we can smell, it then becomes necessary to communicate our perceptions to others or there is no chance of elevating our appreciation of any art form. Verbalising our sensory experiences is the short cut to greater pleasure. But that is easier said than done, without lots of practice.

Children have the benefit of their senses long before they are able to converse – just watch their reaction to good or bad offerings; and it's possible that the smell part of our brain predates useful conversation. Foetal infants have been observed in the uterus responding to tastes of sugar and other compounds. The stone age Fred Flintstone possibly lauded the merits of an underdone dinosaur rib fillet and jungle juice with the odd grunt. Many modern day winelovers have the same tongue tied problem. 'I know what it smells/tastes like but can't explain it!' is an all too frequent response.

Winelovers must start somewhere – here and now is a superb time and place to start correctly articulating our experiences. The fear of making a mistake is possible the main cause of reticence for the tyro taster, so let me hasten to assure you that even the most skilled professional is capable of, and makes, regular goofs – in my own case, about 10 a day!

It is perfectly normal for perceptions to differ from one person to another. We, ourselves, are the only ones who are experts in our own perceptions – if we see red as red/brown and smell chardonnay as grapefruit when others experience apricot, lime or melon, then these are our personal judgments. Where there is no absolute, I think your personal judgment is objective, not subjective as many people like to say. The very reason that there are so many wines on the market, and new styles appearing daily, is that winemakers and marketers wish to provide for all tastes. If there were but one common taste there would be but one common wine. (Ever worse, one restaurant menu.)

Just to prove that you have nothing to fear about articulating your smell experiences, have a look at some of the more regular answers we receive to our tests with common fragrances:

*Strawberry* has been called: Peach, cherry, vanilla, musk, cough medicine, apple juice, jelly beans, rose perfume, chewing gum, caramel, chocolate, mango, pineapple, apricot.

*Ginger* has been called: Soap, three-in-one oil, turpentine, pine-gum, grass, gasoline, onion, rancid butter, lemon citronella, moth balls, cedar, oil of cloves.

*Apricot* has been called: Hard candy, mango, pineapple, Hawaiian punch, peppermint, strawberry, shampoo, orange, gingerbread.

*Lychee* has been called: Musky, cedar, banana, caramel, strawberry, marzipan, toffee, coconut, fairy floss.

Conversely, there is not one fragrance in our repertoire of more than 50 common smells that has not, at sometime, been called strawberry.

So it's worth repeating – I believe, we are pereceive fragrance quite differently and one person's meat can easily be another's poison.

### PRECISION

In New York a few years ago, I was discussing the passionfruit character of a wine when, suddenly, I was asked, 'What is passionfruit?'. Then I realised that this exotic fruit grew only in Australasia and Hawaii and unless winelovers had visited that part of the world they could not relate to this smell. A similar or reverse situation occurred in New Zealand when people spoke about feijoa fragrances in wine – I hadn't previously experienced the smell or taste of this local delicacy.

So it's important when we are articulating our experiences that we use precise terms that can be understood. Such esoterics as 'cuddly', 'cheeky', 'delicate', 'elegant', 'pretentious', don't mean the same to everybody and therefore, are not precise terms and only confuse the people with whom you are trying to communicate. With this great confusion of words besieging us, it has been recognised for a long time that we should have a standard vocabulary for communicating wine perceptions.

I'm indebted to Dr A.C. Noble and Professor Adrienne Lehrer of the University of Arizona for their contributions to the wonderful world of wine, words and wheels.

## ODOURS TO LEARN

As mentioned in this chapter, we receive quite incredible results from smell tests during our seminars. For winelovers wishing to identify (and you can) the smell differences between rose, new mown hay and violet, the first hurdle is to stop calling them room freshener – although this is one of their most common uses. When given the smell of ginger, some people write down bourbon. Why? Because they have ginger ale in their bourbon and ginger is the dominant odour of the mix. (Also, the ice in the drink usually dulls everything else.) These strange results are purely lack of training; remedies have been suggested earlier to help in this regard.

### SMELL INQUISITIVE

During 1984, it was my good fortune to present a series of seminars in California, Hawaii, New Zealand and Australia with Professor Ann C. Noble, a world authority in the smell field. In each new city, while on her daily jog, she would stop to smell any unusual flowers or shrubs. She is smell inquisitive, just as art lovers top to look at paintings, or musiclovers listen attentively to the sounds of music. I'm assured that smell can be as sensuous and rewarding as any other art form.

My work around the globe indicates that the list below includes the necessary odours for the keen enophile (and a must for anyone professionally engaged in the making, distribution or selling of wine) to be able to recognise. And, be assured, it is impossible to have too much practice.

I have presented both fresh blackberry juice and the synthetic blackberry flavour (as used in ice cream, cordial, milk shakes, cakes) in our seminars. Even though it is often identified as a 'berry' smell, not a large percentage of people recognise the blackberry flavour for what it is; not one person in the world has gone close to identifying the real blackberry juice.

Cherry is another odour rarely recognised even though one regularly reads that this wine, or another, has 'overtones of cherry', or a 'cherry-like flavour'. So few people are able to recognise the smell of cherry, that one wonders if these critics know what blackberry or cherry really smell like?

ESSENTIAL ODOURS

Here is a list of chemical, fruit and floral odours to sharpen up your smell skills; of course, there are many more, but these are essential.

| CHEMICAL | |
|---|---|
| Acetic Acid | Vingegary. |
| Acetaldehyde | Distinctive smell of sherry. |
| Ethyl Acetate | Nail polish remover, model aero glue. |
| Diacetyl | Smell mixed into margarine to make it resemble butter; a byproduct of malo-lactic fermentation that gives chardonnay its 'buttery' smell. Also in beer and red wine. |
| Linalool individually and | Floral, citric. |
| Geraniol combined | Distinguishing odours of riesling, muscat and gewurztraminer wines. |
| Hydrogen Sulphide | Rotten egg smell – rotten wine smell also. |
| Sulphur Dioxide | The sulphur smell of a match when lit. |
| Ethyl Alcohol (Ethanol) | |

| FLORAL |
|---|
| Rose, violet, jasmine, geranium. |

| FRUITY |
|---|
| Apples, apricot, peach, raw and cooked; grapefruit, lemon, pinepapple, strawberry, banana, raisin, black currant, prune, fig. |

| HERBS AND SPICES |
|---|
| Cinnamon, cloves, pepper mint. |

| VEGETABLES |
|---|
| Garlic, onion, bell pepper (capsicum), asparagus, green and black olives, mushroom. |

## OLFACTION SUMMARY

Smell is the most important sense in the appraisal of food and beverages and never forget this cardinal rule: be patient, don't rush past the smell appraisal.

The most abundant volatiles are alcohols, aldehydes and esters. Only volatile substances are odorous.

Most individuals perceive and respond differently to the same odour; very few odours can be consdered absolute.

Only a small percentage, about two per cent, of available odour finds its way to the smell receptors. Make the most of it.

Each individual has a different level of smell acuity just as we each have smell 'blind spots'.

Normal breathing brings only a minute percentage of odour into contact with the smell organs. It is necesssary to make a positive sniff, upwards.

Only one sniff is necessary, more than three are confusing.

Close the eyes while smelling to help concentration.

Should your smell mechanism become fatigued smell a glass of water and rest.

Our perceptions of smell differ from one individual to another and we each have a different level of acuity.

Practice, practice, practice on the 'Odours to Learn': chemicals, fruits, flowers, herbs, spices and vegetables.

Use words and language that are easily understood and portable, from one group or place to another, even if it's on the other side of the world.

### APPRAISAL CHECKLIST

Remember, there are four methods of smell appraisal, use them all!

1. External nose.
2. In mouth.
3. Retro-olfactory.
4. Empty glass.

## WORDS THAT SMELL

*Acetaldehyde:* The essential character of sherry, formned by oxidised alcohol.
*Acuity:* Keenness, sharpness.
*Alcohol:* A flammable, volatile, colourless liquid produced by the fermentation of sugars, also called ethyl alcohol and ethanol. A major contributor to smell.
*Aldehyde:* Oxidation of primary alcohols. Important contributor to smell.
*Anosmia:* Loss of the sense of smell.
*Aroma:* The fragrance provided by the grape berry.
*Bouquet:* The part of the 'nose' made up from the winemaking and ageing processes. When combined with 'aroma' becomes the 'nose' of the wine.
*Cilia:* Smell receptors located in the olfactory epithelium.
*Esters:* Organic compounds formed by the union of an acid and an alcohol. With alcohol and aldehydes, form the principal components of smell.
*Fragrance:* A sweet or pleasant odour.
*Hydrogen Sulphide:* Colourless gas formed by decaying vegetable matter. Commonly referred to as $H_2S$ and identified as a rotten egg smell.
*Mercaptans:* A sulphur containing organic compound, commonly used as the smell in natural gas. Has a skunky or garlic smell.

# WINE AROMA WHEEL

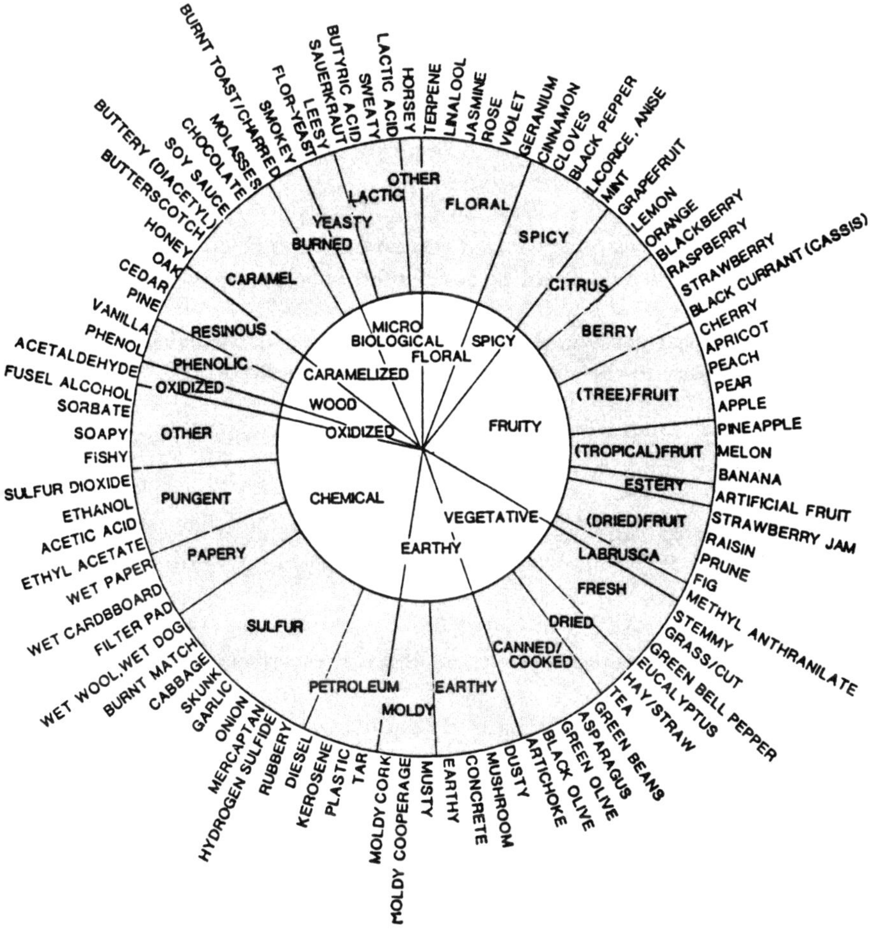

*Nose:* The smell of wine that combines the bouquet and aroma.
*Peptides:* Natural or synthetic compounds containing at least two amino acids. Naturally occurring pituitary hormones.
*Pheromones:* Substances that are excreted externally eliciting a response from another individual of the same species.
*Retro Olfactory:* Or retro nasal. Smelling through the mouth.
*Savour:* The 'smell' when exhaling through the nose.
*Volatile:* Evaporating easily in the form of a vapour – gaseous or in the gas phase.

## OLFACTORY EXERCISE

1. Pour normal evaluation amount, say two ounces, of wine into each of three glasses.
2. Cover each glass with petri dish (or take-out cup lid).
3. Remove lid and smell glass one. Replace lid. Record your impressions of both aroma and bouquet on a score sheet.
4. Revolve glass two in a circular movement, swirling the wine up the glass. This movement coats all sides of the glass and 'opens up' the wine. (Until you learn the idea of this movement, it is best practiced on a flat surface, eg table, counter.) Remove lid from glass after it has been placed under nose. You will notice a much increased volume of odour than was available from glass one.
5. With the lid firmly held on glass three (if no lid available; cup your hand over top of glass) and shake the glass vigorously. Before removing lid or hand place glass under nose. In addition to a much increased volume of odour, it is more than likely that some previously unavailable odours will become evident. This a good method to use if a wine appears to have no obvious olfactory odours (dumb), or if you are in search of particular odours such as $SO_2$ or yeast.

GLASS 1
No movement

GLASS 2
Swirl

GLASS 3
Shake

# OLFACTORY RECORD

These sheets have been designed to cater for all wine styles; as such they cover both generic and varietal wine styles.

PRIOR TO TASTING

*Olfactory*

| | |
|---|---|
| Aroma: | Fruity, floral, spicy, vegetative, earthy. |
| Bouquet: | Clean, fresh, dirty ($H_2S$, mercaptans, etc), yeasty, oak, $SO_2$ (no irritation). |
| Tactile: | $SO_2$, alcohol (irritating). |
| Intensity: | None, light, medium, high. |

## WINE EVALUATION RECORD

INTERNATIONAL WINE ACADEMY

Occasion A.W.S.

Place ROCHESTER Date ____________

| | WINE CHARDONNAY | PRICE | SIGHT 4 MAX | AROMA/ BOUQUET 6 MAX | IN MOUTH 6 MAX | AFTER-TASTE 3 MAX |
|---|---|---|---|---|---|---|
| 1 | CH. LAGNIAPPE 1982 | OH | 3.8 | 4.9 | 5.2 | |
| 2 | BERINGER 1982 | CA | 3.7 | 4.7 | | |
| 3 | K. FRANK 1982 | N.Y. | 3.7 | 4.6 | | |
| 4 | | | | | | |

AROMA AND BOUQUET

| | | |
|---|---|---|
| 6 points | Extraordinary | Unmistakable characteristic aroma of grape variety or wine type. Outstanding and complex bouquet. Exceptional balance of aroma and bouquet. |
| 5 points | Excellent | Characteristic aroma. Complex bouquet. Well balanced. |
| 4 points | Good | Characteristic aroma. Distinguishable bouquet. |
| 3 points | Pleasant | Slight aroma and bouquet, but pleasant. |
| 2 points | Acceptable | No perceptible aroma or bouquet. |
| 1 point | Poor | Rating 3 above with slight off odours. |
| 0 points | Objectionable | Objectionable and offensive off odours. |

Use decimal points or fractions when necessary.

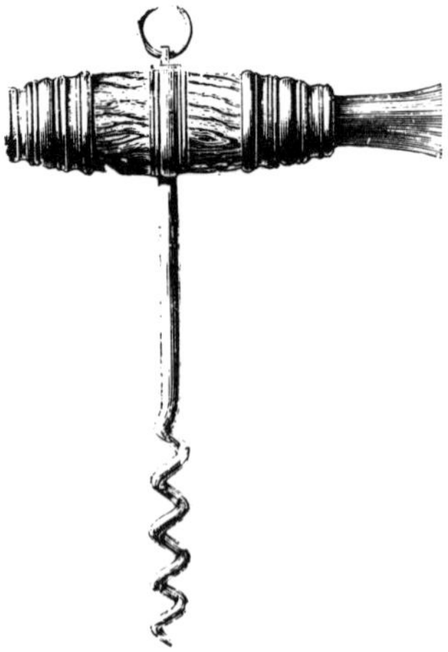

# TASTE – GUSTATION

GUSTATION – the art or faculty of tasting . . .
'perhaps kissing is our civilised way of selecting a mate by taste.'

David Wolsk, Sensory Processes

Precise words are one of the main factors in wine evaluation – so let's start by carefully defining 'taste'. As the word, technically, only applies to the four basic tastes of sugar, sour, salt and bitter, we should use the words 'evaluation' or 'assessment' in place of the misused and misleading generalised 'tasting'. After all, this is a book about sensory evaluation.

## THE LIMITED SENSE

Taste, as such, is a very limited sense due to the physiological makeup of the taste receptors. What we really receive in our mouths is an overall flavour impression. Many people think that when we have a cold we lose our sense of taste. Wrong! We lose our sense of smell; taste is rarely affected.

An apple, potato and onion all smell quite different, but a blindfolded person, deprived of smell, would be hard put to differentiate the taste of these three similarly textured products. Try it next time you have a cold. If, by necessity (or sheer devilment), we were tube fed a superb three course meal from our favourite restaurant, our hungry tummies would taste and smell nothing. What a waste!

So it is of prime concern to the budding sensory evaluator/judge that 'taste' is recognised for what it is – a limited sense; and our efforts should be concentrated in the discrimination of the overall flavour impressions – taste, touch and smell.

I think it is a tragedy that so many influential critics know so little about the interrelation of all the physical senses involved in enjoying wine, and talk indiscriminately about 'taste'. Even worse, many dictate that there is, or should be, a 'common taste' for each product from wine down to even such a mundane commodity as bread. There isn't – and I hope there never will be.

### LEARN ABOUT TASTE

It is thought that the taste insensitivity in humans is brought about because our taste buds are rather unsophisticated by comparison with other animals, and, as individuals, we do ever so little to train any of our senses. For reasons unknown, we teach children about sight and colour, teach them the enjoyment of sound but not about smell or taste.

The lack of knowledge, the difficulty in measuring taste responses (even trained people can only give about 40 per cent accurate response) and the difference between animals used in laboratory tests and human subjects, makes for a lack of positive statements about the taste sense. Bearing that in mind, I'll keep saying 'possibly', 'we believe', 'it is understood' etc because there are so many unanswered questions regarding the senses of taste, touch and smell.

Unlike the smell, sight and hearing receptors, which as primary sensory cells combine the functions of transduction (receiving) and conduction (sending), the taste receptors are not neurons sending their own messages to the brain; they function only as receivers (transducers). This simply means that the other sensory receptors pick up the signal, be it sight, hearing or smell, and the receptor sends that message. With taste, the receptor has to hook onto a neuron to send its message. We believe that taste receptors are continually mobile, degenerating and regenerating and are far fewer in number than the olfactory receptors.

## ORAL CAVITY FRONTAL

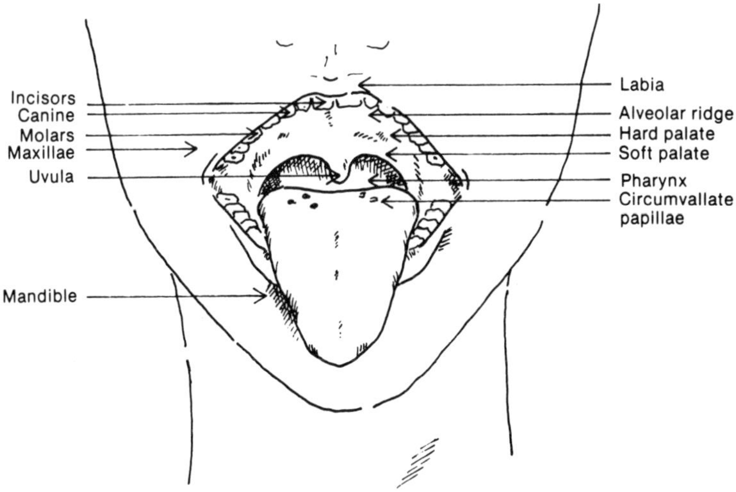


A frontal view of the oral cavity with principal structures labelled.

(From Christensen, C.M. (1984) 'Food Texture Perception' in 'Advances in Food Research' Vol 29, (C.O. Chichester, E.M. Mrak & B.S. Schwergert ets). Academic Press.

## PHYSIOLOGY OF TASTE

The surfaces of the oral cavity, i.e. tongue, soft palate, lips, gums and cheeks (epiglottis and larynx, mainly in children) are covered with four types of papillae (Latin = nipple), this is the roughness of the tongue's surface. Three types contain taste chemo-receptors (taste buds) measuring about .07mm deep and .05mm wide, which are located in the depressions of the papillae.

Unlike the receptors of sight and haring, taste receptors are continually being replaced, some 3000-5000 daily, or a complete change at about weekly intervals. What were once thought to be different sizes and types of taste buds are known to be developing or degenerating receptors. On the positive side, this could be a clever built in safety mechanism because if we burn our tongue the affected taste buds will be replaced within a week. It is now known that we also have a turnover of smell receptors.

The negative side is that this regular movement possibly accounts for our lack of sensivity in taste. Whereas the eye can make some 300 000 comparative judgments, the smell and hearing receptors are super sensitive, we need a 30 per cent increase or decrease in a given substance before the taste threshold can register a difference. A classic example is acetic acid which tastes the same as most other wine acids, yet the smell threshold of ethyl acetate is something like 24 000 times lower than the taste threshold.

# ORAL CAVITY IN PROFILE

H: Hard Palate
L: Lip
S: Soft Palate
T: Teeth

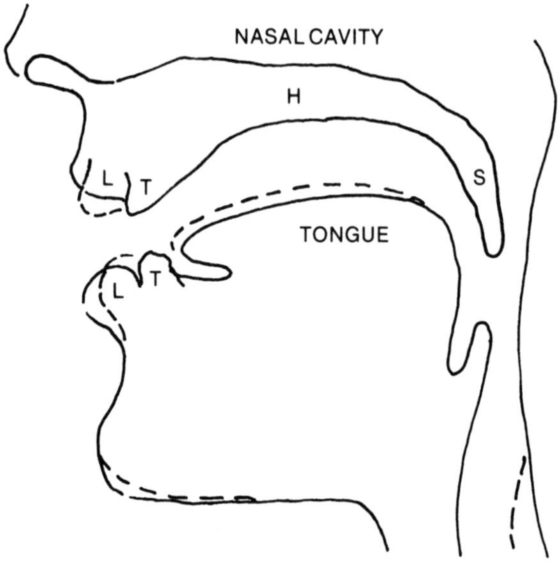


FOUR BASIC TASTES

The common belief (but one no longer enjoying international agreement) is that we have four basic tastes which, although widespread in the oral cavity, are said to be conveniently grouped;

Sugar registering on the tip of the tongue.

Salt impressing the taste buds on either side of, and over the top of, the tongue near the front.

Sour also along the sides of the tongue but further back.

Bitter on the rear top of the tongue.

The bad news is that this is untrue! Extensive research now tells us that these taste sensations are felt with the same sensitivity on all portions of the tongue and other parts of the oral cavity, except bitter which registers more strongly in the back of the mouth. We do not perceive these four tastes simultaneously, rather they become evident one after another.

After experimenting with solutions made up from these components it's possible that you will find these generalisations do vary with the individual. The fact that children lick sugar candy and ice cream with the tip of their tongue, whereas Dad heaves his beer to the rear of his mouth enabling the bitterness of the brew to be perceived, does in some way support the general idea of special areas of taste sensitivity.

## SAPID SUBSTANCES

The perception of sapid (those having taste) substances is somewhat similar to the lock and key principle discussed in the olfaction chapter. These sapid substances have both mineral and organic backgrounds. Electrophysiological (laboratory tests using electrical pulses) recordings of the potential from single taste cells shows that they are sensitive to more than one basic substance, with different cells having different patterns of relative sensitivities. The taste buds, apparently, code preferentially rather than individually. Although smell molecules have a habit of 'hanging around', taste molecules are easily washed away, with the exception of bitter compounds and the sweetener aspartame.

There is little question that each person's 'palate' (I hate that word) is as individual as is his or her pulse beat or fingerprints. Temperature plays a key role in these taste responses and is discussed at length in the following chapter on the tactile sense.

The taste sense becomes active early in our life. Babies (even before birth) immediately respond to sugar, salt, lemon juice and quinine which stimulate the four accepted taste areas. Babies seem to like sweet tastes – maybe mother's milk shapes this affinity – but dislike the rest. By the time we reach adulthood most people grow to accept salty and sour tastes but, in terms of consumers, it is mainly the beer drinkers who acquire any taste for bitterness, even though a lot of coffee could be considered bitter. Such perception of bitterness could be a relative cultural idiosyncrasy. I personally find most American coffee excessively bitter. In fact, I find it hard to obtain a good cup of coffee in the USA. Americans who taste the Australian national breakfast phenomenon Vegemite or Marmite (two brand names) find this popular spread far too salty, yet most Australians would not consider it so. It's a general belief that poisonous natural foods (berries, leaves and roots) are known to be bitter, whereas sweet things in the wild tend to be life sustaining.

The mouth is, almost continually, lubricated through sets of glands that open into various parts of the cavity. These glands are known as parotid, sublingual and submandibular. Without saliva we would have no taste, only the sense of touch.

The taste receptors respond to substances dissolved in the oral fluids (saliva) bathing them, and the importance of the chemical composition of the saliva in our mouth has yet to be properly understood. One popular theory suggests that the sodium level of saliva varies quite markedly during the course of a day. Aside from psychological factors, this I believe, accounts for similar glasses of wine having what appears to be a different taste in the morning and evening, or from one day to another. It is pleasing to note that research work is continuing on the fascinating subject of the chemical makeup of the saliva. There is no doubt in my mind that this, more than anything else, accounts for the differences in our taste preferences. However, we do know that our taste threshold lowers considerably when we rinse our mouth with distilled water. We are then able to perceive basic tastes at lesser concentrations.

### SALIVA

As mentioned above, we are all different in our perception and taste thresholds of wine components; it is recommended that you carefully record the impressions of the various components on your teeth, gums, cheeks and the rest of the oral cavity. With training, we are able to perceive three different threshold levels, over and above a blank sample of distilled water.

1. The minimum concentration is referred to as the 'detection' threshold.
2. The next stage is the 'identification' threshold where we can both detect and identify the substance.
3. Being able to quantify the substance is the 'difference' threshold.

At all times be conscious of the difference between the four basic tastes and the tactile senses of hot/cold, rough/smooth, pain/irritation, oily.

## COMPONENTS OF TASTE

Let's move on and have a look at each of these basic tastes in detail.

### ACIDS

Of all wine components, natural fruit acids, which make wine sour and different from other beverages, are the most important contributors to the life, balance and refinement of wine. Apart from their flavour benefits, acids also protect wine from spoilage. However, there are two groups of acids involved in wine, mineral and organic. In food and beverages mineral acids are only in minute traces if at all, and are noted for their aggressiveness. These are sulphuric, nitric and hydrochloric. The organic acids are malic, tartaric, citric and lactic.

These can be further broken down into groups by origin. Acids that originate in the grape berry are the natural fruit acids – malic, tartaric and citric. Then there are the acids that originate during fermentation and through microbiological reaction during evolution or maturation – lactic, acetic, succinic, formic, propionic to name a few of the more important ones. These acids are important contributors to wine aroma.

Malic and tartaric are the main acids of wine while citric, lactic and others which are in limited quanitities, assist with flavour and balance. Malic acid occurs in many fruits including grapes, apples and gooseberries. Tartaric is mainly a grape acid and is known to dominate in warm viticultural area fruit; malic acid seems to predominate in cooler areas. The longer, slower ripening conditions in cool climates apparently inhibits malic acid respiration from the berry.

It is unfortunate that acid is classified in the sour/salt taste groupings. While acid does certainly contribute to sourness, the terms acid and sour have totally different connotations in wine evaluation language. Crisp, clean acidity gives wine life and lightness whereas sourness, as such, is very much a negative term.

When discussing acidity in wine, pH (p for power, H for hydrogen ion concentration) always rears its head. pH, as mentioned in the colour chapter, is all important in wine quality but is more applicable to winemaking than wine evaluation.

## THE pH FACTOR

pH is an expression of hydrogen ion concentration in solution. An ion is an atom which has an electrical charge and is not bound to another atom. The pH scale ranges from 1-14. pH 7 is neutral; pure distilled water is pH 7 or neutral. Below pH 7 a solution moves toward acidity, above pH 7 the solution is alkaline. (pH measurements are commonly used to determine garden soil acid/alkaline levels and this soil balance can have a strong influence on grape juice pH.) Above 3.8 wine has so little acid that it is flat, between 3.2 and 3.6 wine is microbiologically stable; lemon juice is about 2.3, and 0 is total acidity.

Winemakers look for figures between pH 3.00 and pH 4.00. Generally the lower the pH figure the higher the acidity, but winemakers are often frustrated by high pH and high acid in some viticultural areas, usually those with high potassium in the soil.

Desirable pH levels in wine are:

| | |
|---|---|
| White table wines | pH 3.00 - 3.40 |
| (A light style wine, i.e. riesling is more likely to be near pH 3.00 wheareas a fuller bodied wine, i.e. chablis or chardonnay would be at the higher end.) | |
| Red table wines | pH 3.30 - 3.60 |
| Dessert wines | pH 3.50 - 3.80 |

Relativity is the dominant factor about pH. Low pH factors will give light bodied wines such as the classic rieslings of the Mosel, Rhine and New York State. But this low figure is relative to the winegrowing region – and the wine style. Take as an example cabernet and riesling wines from the cool regions of Bordeaux (France) and Rheingau (Germany) and compare them with those from the warm inland irrigated areas of California or Australia.

The French and German wines must have figures of 3.3-3.5 and 3.0-3.2 respectively to retain their classic styles, whereas in the warmer regions a cabernet at 3.5 pH and a riesling at 3.4 would still be considered excellent wines. This is because warm area fruit attains a degree of ripeness beyond the capabilities of cool areas and ripe fruit provides wine of 'fuller body'.

Even where the grape variety is constant, the style varies enormously within a climatic region. In Bordeaux where a Medoc red may have a pH reading of 3.5 the sweet white table wines of Sauternes or Barsac with pH readings in excess of 3.6 will command astronomical prices ten times that of the red. As already mentioned, a riesling from the Rhine will be 3.1 pH yet a superb sweet red from the Duoro Valley in Portugal will be 3.6. It is of paramount importance, therefore, that we aren't carried away with low figures for the sake of low figures; what we are looking for is relatively low figures.

Cool seasons or cold climate viticulture, as a general rule, produce grapes with naturally lower pH readings and these wines are associated with fresher and more floral flavours. Winemakers can, and regularly do, legally adjust pH by the addition of acids, normally tartaric or sometimes citric acid. (I know of a case where sulphuric acid was used; beware of Mexican wines!)

Low pH makes numerous other valuable contributions to wine flavour, including stability and prevention of spoilage. Generally, low pH inhibits bacterial spoilage (including malolactic bacteria), as most micro organisms associated with wine have definite chemical limits for activity. For the fuller bodied chardonnays to undergo malolactic fermentation (to produce the complex style of some California wines), one criterion is a higher pH level, usually, but not necessarily, above 3.4. Still further, low pH wines require less $SO_2$ to prevent spoilage of flavour and colour. Work done at UC Davis suggests that in a wine of pH 3.0, 61 per cent of the free $SO_2$ is in molecular form but as the pH increases to 3.3, the molecular $SO_2$ is reduced to 3.1 per cent of the amount of the free $SO_2$ present. The 'bound' sulphur can noticably contribute to a lack of fruit flavour in the wine.

So much for pH – let's have a look at the acids.

## ACID IN MATURE FRUIT

As fruit matures on the vine, a certain amount of chemical 'musical chairs' takes place. Initially the young berry has a high content of malic acid which is retained in cool climates but respired in warm climate viticulture allowing tartaric to become the dominant acid. This respiration of malic acid decreases total acidity and increases pH. The primary fermentation (converting grape juice to wine) doesn't much alter the overall acid level. The secondary or malolactic fermentation produces lactic acid; as much as 30 per cent of malic is converted to lactic acid at this time.

Lactic acid is associated with milk products (from the decomposition of lactose) including cheese and, along with diacetyl, it accounts for the 'buttery' and 'cheesey' descriptors sometimes given to chardonnay wines (particularly of Californian origin) that have undergone malolactic fermenation and, more importantly, in cabernet sauvignon red table wines from cool areas, that need acid reduction.

## TOTAL ACIDITY

Total acidity is yet another wine term that doesn't mean what it says – it does not include carbonic acid. The term is regularly interchanged with titratable acidity, with which it is not identical, hence it's very confusing. Really, total acidity isn't total acidity at all, and is a term that could well be dropped. While it is still with us, the normal range of total acidity, by definition, is 5-7 g/l red wines, 6-9 g/l for whites, measured as tartaric acid. Beware of the French, they measure in grams per litre of sulphuric acid.

## TITRATABLE ACID

Titratable acid is what gives wine its acid taste – in addition to pH. Titration is a chemical process for determining, in wine, the amount of acid present and is achieved by adding sodium hydroxide to a wine sample until a reaction takes place. The amount of titratable acid is expressed as grams per litre or percentage of volume. Tartaric is the standard in the USA and Australia – sulphuric in France.

## VOLATILE ACID

Volatile acids or VA as they are more often referred to amongst the wine fraternity can be either a plus or a minus, depending on the concentration. It is often said that some top ranking wines owe their greatness to 'controlled' amounts of VA. This is said to give them 'lift' or extra life during the olfactory and in mouth evaluations. The main volatile acid is acetic acid. In a positive sense, trace amounts of VA will add a plus dimension to the wine – in larger doses it is easily detectable as a 'vinegary' character – a damning minus.

## ACETIC EXERCISE

Adding vinegar or acetic acid with a dropper to a glass of ordinary 'jug' wine is a worthwhile exercise at home. Add a drop or two – smell and taste the wine – add a few more drops, smell and taste until the vinegar smell becomes offensive. This is a good way to learn about 'lift', 'volatility' and 'acetification'.

Acids that are steam distillable are considered volatile acids. Beside acetic acid others found in wine are butyric, formic and propionic. Even more important, is ethyl acetate which is formed from acetic acid and ethanol and has a far lower smell threshold than acetic acid.

Historically, microbiological spoilage of wine was considered the main cause of high levels of acetic acid but in recent times it has been found that strains of certain fermentation yeasts have produced acetic acid in undesirable quantities. This is more common in white wine production methods employing low temperatures and clarified juice.

## ACID TEST

In my classes I teach the discrimination of acids by the following exercise which is recommended to every winelover. Purchase from your local home winemaker supply store or grocer a packet each of tartaric and citric acid. To make up a loaded solution of each acid, mix a half teaspoon of crystals in a little warm water (helps dissolve the crystals), then add cold water to make up a litre. Each taster needs one or two ounces of solution, so if you're going solo, two pinches will suffice in four ounces of water. You will need this amount of solution for further mixes. To determine your personal threshold, for these and other solutions, you will need four glasses. Take one half of the solution (two ounces) and add an equal amount (two ounces) of water for mix two (mix one being the base mix). Then take half of mix two and add an equal amount of water for mix three. Glass four should be blank water sample.

Do not keep the acid solutions overnight. Start with solution one and register your perceptions on the record sheet below. Rinse your mouth, preferably with distilled water, between solutions. Following a rest period, try working upwards from the blank sample until reaching the detection threshold.

Another worthwhile training exercise is the triangular test – two blank samples and either sample two or three. You will need an assistant to juggle the glasses around so you don't know which is the odd one or whether the odd one is solution two or three. This is a first class method of learning your detection threshold and the identification and difference thresholds.

You will probably note that as a solution is diluted, the perception of the taste sensations will vary, or move from one area of the mouth to another. In my own case, the strong solution of acid registers on the teeth, gums and lips whereas the weakest solution registers mainly on the tongue. (Strong solutions of sugar and bitterness can be mouthfilling, yet the weak solutions may register on more conventional areas, the tip and rear of the tongue respectively.)

Malic and lactic acids are not easy to find. Try your friendly pharmacist but if all else fails an unripe green apple will suffice for malic acid.

You will taste in the solutions that the acid plus water mixtures are lighter in 'body' than a blank water sample. For permanent reference be sure to write down where these acids register in your mouth, or use the acid record sheet below. I believe, although some disagree, that all acids have different intensities, duration and placement. Tartaric may be noted on the top front of the tongue and leaves a sensation similar to fur on the top teeth. Citric acid may seem fresher and coarser in structure and goes half way along the top of the tongue. Some tasters think citric acid lingers longer. The hard and assertive malic acid, which has been likened to 'licking the side of a battleship', registers on the top and bottom of the tongue, and is often confused with alcohol. You may perceive malic as a green apple taste. Lactic acid, which is much softer and is often difficult to perceive, has been described as 'cheesey' or 'buttery' by some tasters.

Succinic acid has a more salty, rather than acid, taste and can be bitter at the same time.

ACID WORDS

| NEGATIVE – Too Little | POSITIVE | NEGATIVE – Too Much |
|---|---|---|
| Bland | Tart | Acetic |
| Flabby | Crisp | Sour |
| Flat | Piquant | Sharp |
| | Lively | Hard |
| | Zestful | Biting |
| | Tangy | Pricked |
| | | Assertive |

## SUGAR

Amongst winelovers, professional and tyro, the words sweet and sugar are often unwisely used and convey entirely wrong impressions. Many wines are sweet and fruity without being perceived on the tip of the tongue, the conventional area where many people register sugar. The muscat family is an example – even the driest (dry = without sugar) muscat wine can appear to contain sugar, yet it is really the fruitiness of the variety that is 'mouth filling' and it will not register on the tongue tip.

Such wines are suitably for diabetics and the diet conscious. For the purpose of this section sugar is defined as crystalline carbohydrates, mainly glucose and fructose. While the ratio of these sugars varies from wine to wine, it is generally considered that they exist in about equal proportions in all wine. Both are present in many fruit juices and honey.

Fructose is considered to have double the sweetness of cane sugar.

Glucose, the sugar of our blood, is also present in many plants.

Glycerol and alcohols, both produced by fermenting grape sugars, are major contributors to sweetness and are discussed in the sweetness section of the tactile chapter.

There are exceptions that prove the rule, but it could be fairly said that all wines – regardless of their nomenclature – do contain some sugar. Brut de brut (the driest of the dry) champagne style 'bubblies' have cane sugar added. Sparkling wines labelled 'brut' may contain up to 1.5 per cent sugar by volume,

## ACID RECORD CHART

Record your perception of this component with an X on a scale of 10 (mark with x)

| | | WEAK | MODERATE | STRONG |
|---|---|---|---|---|
| | | 1 2 3 | 4 5 6 7 | 8 9 10 |
| Teeth | Upper | . . . | . . . . | . . . |
| | Lower | . . . | . . . . | . . . |
| Gums | Upper | . . . | . . . . | . . . |
| | Lower | . . . | . . . . | . . . |
| Lips | Upper | . . . | . . . . | . . . |
| | Lower | . . . | . . . . | . . . |
| Tongue | Tip | . . . | . . . . | . . . |
| | Top | . . . | . . . . | . . . |
| | Sides | . . . | . . . . | . . . |
| Cheeks | Front | . . . | . . . . | . . . |
| | Rear | . . . | . . . . | . . . |
| Throat | | . . . | . . . . | . . . |
| Roof of mouth | | . . . | . . . . | . . . |

## MAIN ACIDS IN WINE

| ORGANIC ACIDS | ORIGIN | COMMENTS |
|---|---|---|
| *Citric* | Grape berry | Only low quantities – dissipates during fermentation. Common in citrus fruits. |
| *Malic* | Grape berry | Prominent in most fruit and plant life. Metabolises easily – diminishes during ripening and fermentation. Converts to lactic acid during malo-lactic fermentation. It's the 'hard' acid in green apples. |
| *Tartaric* | Grape berry | A specific grape/wine acid. It is the most abundant and strongest acid in wine. If attacked by lactic bacteria it produces both lactic and volatile acidity. |
| *Acetic* | Primary ferment & acetic bacteria | Formed by acetic bacteria, also from yeasts in the primary fermentation and by bacteria in malo-lactic ferments. |
| *Lactic* | Primary and malo-lactic fermentation | Not in grapes. Created in a similar manner to acetic acid during primary and malo-lactic ferments. Associated with dairy products. |
| *Succinic* | From yeast during primary fermentation | Not in grapes – a very stable acid that can be bitter. |

'natur' champagnes are the exceptions, having no added sugar.

There are two simple reasons for this sugar content in wine. The first and obvious one being that it is technically impossible to ferment all the sugar from grape juice – and these are non-fermentable sugars. Secondly, the average consumer does not like naturally dry or very dry products. Brandy and sherry are other examples of naturally dry beverages that have some sweetening agent added to create a more pleasing flavour. Not only is cane sugar added to sweeten brandy but caramel (burnt sugar) is, in many cases, added to provide uniform colour in both brandy and whisky. In some cases, grape juice concentrate (jeropiga) is added to sherry as a sweetener.

## RESIDUAL SUGAR

Modern technology allows the winemaker scope to control the amount of natural grape sugar left in the wine during fermentation. Any amount retained is called residual sugar. It is important for communication and a clear understanding that we are positive about the terms residual and non-fermentable.

Dryness is a comparative term but in white table wines sugar begins to be perceivable at about 0.4 per cent by volume. In red wines the sugar level needs to reach about 1.5 per cent because of the masking effect of tannins. The balance of sugar and acid is vital in sensory evaluation as high sugar or acid levels tend to hide each other, in addition to fatiguing the sense receptors.

It is interesting to note that some US winemakers are experimenting with late harvest (high sugar) red table wines by not fully completing the primary fermentation, thereby leaving some residual sugar in the finished red wine. This revolutionary approach flies in the face of conventional dry red table wine; but why must we always have dry red table wines?

Our modern cuisine is far removed from the food styles that traditionally accompanied dry reds. Sugar gives wine body as well as sweetness and many of us know dishes that scream out for a full bodied, slightly sweet red. Lambrusco, that slightly effervescent and sweet north Italian red wine, surely must rank as one of the world's popular wines, so, who is the 'authority' that dictates that we can't have medium to full bodied sweet red table wines? That all time American favourite 'hearty burgundy', also happens to have one to two per cent residual sugar.

If a winelover doesn't like this style there's no obligation to drink it (he or she would be a lot better person if they chose to give it a fair trial in its right context). One thing is sure, he or she is not going to learn anything from ignoring the style, or from summary dismissal.

Many of the world's great sweet white table wines evolved in Germany, considered the home of the riesling wine style and, originally, gewurztraminer as well. (Alsace, France is now considered the centre for gewurztraminer.) But Germany, like the Champagne region, is the northern limit where grapes will ripen and seasons vary widely. While lesser wine categories like tafelwein, Qualitatswein bestimmter Anbaugebiet (QbA) may have sugar added to the fermentation (a process called chapitalisation), the Qualitatswein mit Pradikat (QmP = wines with special attributes) classification forbids this practice.

The QmP classifications are: Kabinett, Spatlese, Auslese, Beerenauslese, Trockenbeerenauslese. To qualify for these titles, the German Wine Laws 1971 require that the 'must' contains a minimum amount of natural sugar. The measurement is known as Ochsle (pronounced Erks-la) for the nineteenth century founder of the scale, Ferdinand Ochsle. Briefly, Ochsle relates to specific gravity. The following table for the Rheingau, one of the 11 pronounced German wine regions, is indicative of standards of Ochsle required for QmP wines made from the riesling grape variety: Kabinett – 73, Spatlese – 85, Auslese – 95, Beerenauslese – 125, Trockenbeerenauslese – 150.

MUST CONVERSION CHART –
USA, NEW ZEALAND, AUSTRALIA, FRANCE

| SPECIFIC GRAVITY | OCHSLE (GERMAN) | BAUME (FRENCH/AUST) | BRIX (USA/NZ) | APPROX % ALCOHOL (V/V) |
|---|---|---|---|---|
| 1.070 | 70 | 9.4 | 17.0 | 8.8 |
| 1.075 | 75 | 10.1 | 18.1 | 9.4 |
| 1.080 | 80 | 10.7 | 19.3 | 10.0 |
| 1.085 | 85 | 11.3 | 20.4 | 10.6 |
| 1.090 | 90 | 11.9 | 21.5 | 11.3 |
| 1.095 | 95 | 12.5 | 22.5 | 11.9 |
| 1.100 | 100 | 13.1 | 23.7 | 12.5 |
| 1.105 | 105 | 13.7 | 24.8 | 13.1 |
| 1.110 | 110 | 14.3 | 25.8 | 13.8 |

There are individual standards for all 11 regions, and for all varieties including red and white grapes.

The grape varieties riesling, gewurztraminer and muscat are closely related, particularly in fragrance, and are considered to be aromatic varieties. Much of their highly 'floral' aroma comes from the terpine alcohols linalool, nerol and geraniol – look for these at 12 o'clock on the Aromo Wheel (page ??). These highly scented wines appear to be unbalanced if made in the naturally dry style (when all grape sugar is converted to alcohol) and most winemakers agree that these wines benefit from some residual sugar to give the wine balance of flavour and body.

While there are many superb sweet white table wines made in the USA, Australia and other wine producing nations, the classic styles are from the French regions of Barsac and Sauternes (made from the grape varieties semillon and sauvignon), the Hungarian style tokay made with furmint grapes and the German styles mentioned above.

## SUGAR EXERCISES

Make up 'loaded sugar and water solutions by adding a heaped dessertspoon of sugar to a glass of water. Then make up the three mixes and the blank water sample as explained under acids on page 67. Write on your record sheet where the sugar registers in the mouth. Observe the difference in the viscosity or 'body' of the number one solution. Note how it lies in your mouth, rather limply and has a 'cloying' finish.

Now you are ready for a triangular test with the sugar solutions.

Combine equal amounts of the number one tartaric acid and water solution with the number one sugar and water solution and see how acid brings the solution to 'life', lightens the 'body' and makes the finish much crisper by removing the 'cloying' nature of the sugar. The sugar solution gives viscosity or 'body' to the acid and water solution.

### SUGAR WORDS

| NEGATIVE – TOO LITTLE | POSITIVE | NEGATIVE – TOO MUCH |
|---|---|---|
| Lacking | Sweet | Syrupy |
| Watery | Semi-sweet | Cloying |
| Thin | Semi-dry | Rounded |
| | | Balanced |

## SUGAR RECORD CHART

Record your perception of these components on a scale of 10

| | | WEAK | MODERATE | STRONG |
|---|---|---|---|---|
| | | 1 2 3 | 4 5 6 7 | 8 9 10 |
| Teeth | Upper | . . . | . . . . | . . . |
| | Lower | . . . | . . . . | . . . |
| Gums | Upper | . . . | . . . . | . . . |
| | Lower | . . . | . . . . | . . . |
| Lips | Upper | . . . | . . . . | . . . |
| | Lower | . . . | . . . . | . . . |
| Tongue | Tip | . . . | . . . . | . . . |
| | Top | . . . | . . . . | . . . |
| | Sides | . . . | . . . . | . . . |
| Cheeks | Front | . . . | . . . . | . . . |
| | Rear | . . . | . . . . | . . . |
| Throat | | . . . | . . . . | . . . |
| Roof of mouth | | . . . | . . . . | . . . |

## SUGAR/ACID MIX RECORD CHART

Record your perception of these components on a scale of 10

| | | WEAK | MODERATE | STRONG |
|---|---|---|---|---|
| | | 1 2 3 | 4 5 6 7 | 8 9 10 |
| Teeth | Upper | . . . | . . . . | . . . |
| | Lower | . . . | . . . . | . . . |
| Gums | Upper | . . . | . . . . | . . . |
| | Lower | . . . | . . . . | . . . |
| Lips | Upper | . . . | . . . . | . . . |
| | Lower | . . . | . . . . | . . . |
| Tongue | Tip | . . . | . . . . | . . . |
| | Top | . . . | . . . . | . . . |
| | Sides | . . . | . . . . | . . . |
| Cheeks | Front | . . . | . . . . | . . . |
| | Rear | . . . | . . . . | . . . |
| Throat | | . . . | . . . . | . . . |
| Roof of mouth | | . . . | . . . . | . . . |

### BITTERNESS

Historically, humans and animals have been well served by nature as nearly all poisonous food plants, berries and roots are bitter. Excessive bitterness is possibly the most universally disliked component of all foods and beverages.

Bitterness in food and beverages comes from two sources – vegetable extracts and chemical salts. The vegetable extracts are: cassia, gentian, quinquina and nux vomica. Potassium iodide, potassium sulphate, sodium iodide, magnesium chloride, calcium chloride and quinine sulphate are some of the salts providing bitterness.

During bacterial decomposition, glycerin becomes acrolein and by combining with the polyphenols becomes bitter. Yet, as a basic taste response even the sweetest wine should have some bitterness, even if it's below the perceivable threshold – just as the driest wine will have sugar, also below perceptability. It's my strong belief that nearly all food and beverages should contain a measurable amount of each of the four basic tastes to provide balance and complexity. The subject is further discussed with astringency in the tactile chapter.

Over the years the word 'bitter' has been synonymous with lager and ale. Maybe these brewed beverages are bitter – to my personal taste most US and Australian beers are decidedly sweet in the mouth, with an unpleasant bitter aftertaste. Maybe my palate is fooling me, but, the sweetness level of beer has apparently increased considerably in the past decade – or is it that I do not like sweet beverages? I think not, as I have an intense love of sweet table and fortified wines.

Strong black coffee, tea, tonic water, soluble asprin are everyday examples of bitterness. For the majority of people bitterness and astringency are an acquired taste or it is a matter of building up tolerance to them. On the positive side bitterness does have an important role (albeit that of a poor relative) in many wine styles, particularly dry reds and the drier fortified wines.

Bitterness, in wine, is a product of phenolic extractions (along with colour) from the grape skins, seeds and stems. This also contributes to astringency. As such, bitterness is born in the first week of the wine's life – from the first moment the grapes are 'damaged' either by mechanical harvesting or crushed at the winery. As winemaking and associated grape harvesting methods differ enormously between large and small producers, it's impossible to come out in favour of any particular technique. While many producers around the world pick one bunch of grapes at a time, an increasing number are using several mechanical harvesters turning in 30 tons an hour. Both methods of harvesting can have a dramatic impact on bitterness.

As we move further into the 1980s, an increasing number of small producers are crushing grapes in the vineyard rather than transporting them to the winery, whereas larger producers using mechanical harvesters can be despatching gondolas of berries many miles or hours to the processing point. Two critical factors during this part of processing are skin-juice contact and temperature.

Most grapes in the northern hemisphere are picked in the fall – although some are harvested as early as July, others not until November. Hot weather and travel, have a definite influence on high berry/must temperature – high temperature in turn is the very essence of increased pH and phenolic extraction and bitterness as demonstrated by a sample of grapes tested in Missouri: at 48°F – pH 3.20; at 59°F – ph 3.37; at 66°F – pH 3.45; at 80°F – the pH blew out to 3.47.

The small grape vineyardist has several methods to combat these problems – and, fortunately, so has the larger producer. Unlike human grape pickers, mechanical grape harvesters can, and do work through the cool night hours. So much so that a leading Californian sparkling wine producer with a specialist interest in premium wine quality, has come out in favour of the mechanical method: a decision not reached lightly.

### BITTERNESS EXERCISE

Make up a bitter solution by doubling the strength of your normal cup of tea or coffee – doesn't the thought make you shudder? If you can obtain 50 mg of quinine sulphate from your friendly pharmacist, mix it with four ounces of water and you will have the same bitter mix used in laboratory tests.

## HEAT SUMMATION

This book deliberately endeavoured to keep away from the technical aspect of winemaking. Yet if the winelover is to reach his or her full potential as a judge of wine, there are some matters of viticulture and enology that should be understood.

The following reprint from my book *An Encounter with Wine* covers the subject of heat summation and provides an understanding of the part played by climate and geography which is pertinent to this chapter.

Heat summation is the standard technique used in comparing and assessing the almost infinite permutations of climatic and geographical features that make up any wine appellation. Basically it is a way of ensuring one of the most critical elements of viticulture – the amount of heat involved in the growing and ripening processes of the fruit. Vines don't like being too close to the equator or the poles. Other than these obvious points of latitude, there are three major factors affecting the amount of heat provided to the vines: water, soil, elevation.

### WATER

Many of the classical wine areas are on slopes close to large bodies of water, which store heat during the day and release it at night thus giving the vines a desirable evenness of temperature. One thinks of Germany's Rhine Valley, France's Valley of the Marne, or of Bordeaux, between the Atlantic Ocean and the Gironde River.

Winegrowers around the Finger Lakes of New York State, and the regions bordering Lake Erie, are very conscious of the impact of these large water bodies in equalising temperatures. (Many Californian regions have a maritime influence, particularly the ones where, almost daily, fogs roll in from the Pacific.) This factor is of little importance in Australia, where, except for vines along the Murray River (and a few in Tasmania and Western Australia), most vines are well removed from any large lakes or rivers.

### SOIL

A second factor affecting the vines micro climate is stony soil, which, like water bodies, stores heat during the day and thus contributes to diurnal evenness between day and night temperatures.

## ELEVATION

The third factor is elevation. Obviously, the higher we go above sea level the cooler the climate. Many of Australia's vineyards are situated around the Great Dividing Range which forms the spine of the eastern states, from northern Queensland to Great Western in Victoria, in much the same way as the Appalachians spear down the eastern side of the United States.

## VINEYARD SITING

After sleeping all winter the vines come to life with the first flush of spring warmth, when the temperature reaches a mean daily average of 50 degrees F (10C). Depending on the heat summation and the grape variety, the new fruit will be ready for harvesting anytime from 90 and 190 days after budburst. This is a great range of harvest seasons, especially when some areas have only 120 days of frost free growing time. Thus it is vital that vignerons have the right varieties planted in the right areas (particularly when, in Australia and the USA, they have a minimum of 80 varieties to choose from).

They are helped in this decision by a valuable guide to vineyard selection developed some years ago by researchers at the University of California, Davis. The technique is called 'degree days' or 'heat summation' and is obtained by totalling the number of degrees above a mean of 50°F for each day of the growing season, which in Australia, is considered to be from October 1 to April 30.

In the northern hemisphere the period is from April 1 to October 30. Thus if the temperature today is 80°F we deduct 50 and have 30 heat units for the day. These heat units are added for each day of the growing season to arrive at the heat summation. Grapes need a minimum of 1700 such units to have any chance of ripening, and a maximum of 5200, above which they aren't even any use for curry.

The viticultural areas of the world have been classified into five levels of heat summation. Australia and North America are represented in all five. Some comparative examples will quickly suggest the wide viticultural (and therefore winemaking) choices available in these countries.

Regions one and two are ideally suited to making light dry table wines of distinction as the fruit ripens late in the season allowing maximum flavour build up. In the warmer region three, fruit fully ripens earlier providing wines with more body.

Grapes that mature quickly produce wines suitable for drinking at a young age (including a lot of bulk wines for jugs and casks). These wines come from warmer area regions four and five which are also known for their excellent ports and brandies.

All this is generalisation, as the most expensive sweet table wines come from region one and two, and some splendid and expensive table wines come from regions four and five. Consequently, critics of the degree day heat measurement scheme say that it is inaccurate. But it was only ever meant to be a guide and one of the many factors to be considered in vineyard site selection.

However, a study of picking dates for the grape variety riesling in the USA and Australia would clearly justify this system and, if used wisely, it can be a very accurate tool.

## HEAT SUMMATION °F DEGREE DAYS

See table on page 78

## IN MOUTH PROFILES

Not only do we have a need for a hedonic point score, we also need to determine what makes one riesling, chardonnay or cabernet different to other wines in the flight. ('Flight' – a group of wines presented for evaluation.)

This in mouth profiling is the first simple step. Later in our work we will combine olfactory and in mouth profiling.

Each 'spoke' of the wheel represents a scale of 1-10, one being nearest the centre and representing low intensity. Ten is on the outside of the spoke and represent high intensity.

*Wine No 1:* Sugar not applicable to this wine style. Young (2-3 years old), cool climate, region 1-2, dry red. High acid, medium oak, high grape tannin, moderate to high alcohol, dormant fruit. Reasonably high alcohol and tannin gives high viscosity, balance just above moderate due to high acid, alcohol and low fruit. As this wine develops with bottle maturation (evolution) the latent fruit will be enhanced and the other components will combine to give the wine good balance. Because of its good fruit, acid and tannin, this wine is a good long term cellaring prospect, more than eight years from vintage date.

WINE ONE

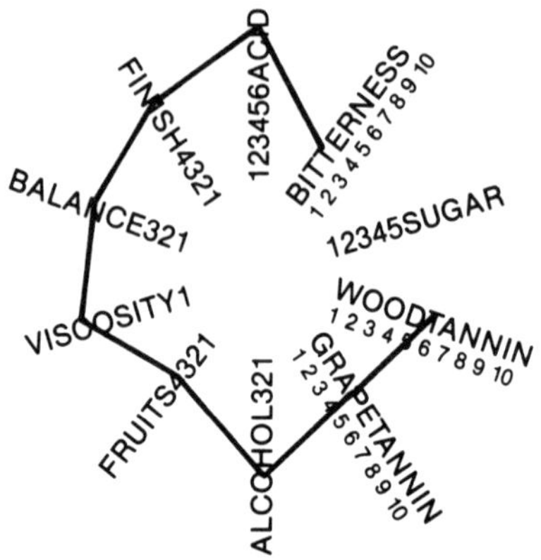

*Wine No 2:* Regions 3-4, dry red 3-4 years old. Less acid, touch more oak as the winemaker believed the ripe fruit could hold more. At this time a better balanced wine than No 1 and softer finish. Good medium term cellaring wine, 5-8 years from vintage date.

WINE TWO

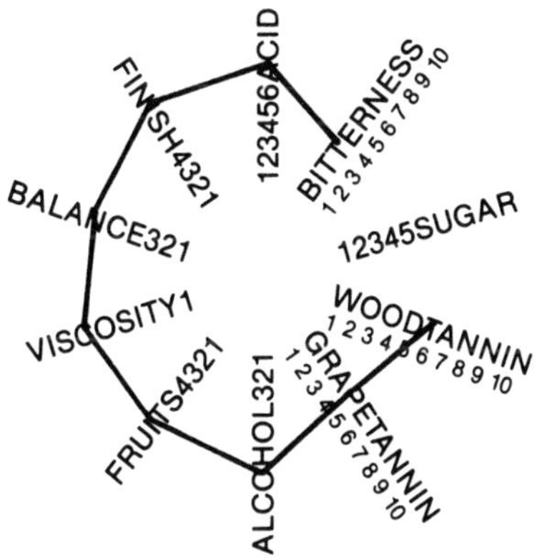


*Wine No 3:* Top class aged dry red from regions 1-3, say 8-10 years old. Approaching its peak, with a long time to run. Shows all the benefits of evolution in a good cellar; everything in balance.

WINE THREE

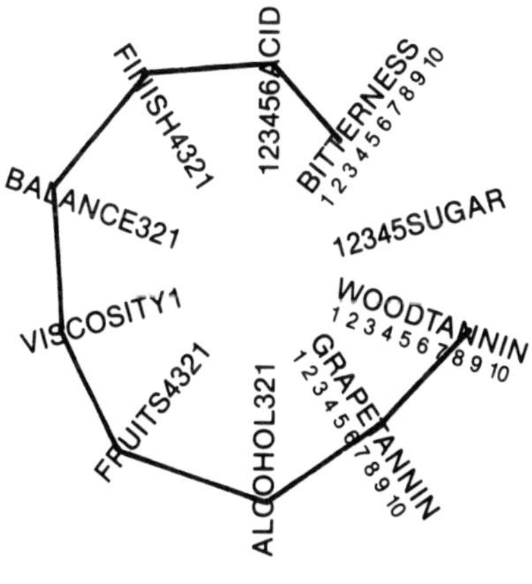

# HEAT SUMMATION °F DEGREE DAYS

## REGION ONE

| | | |
|---|---|---|
| Rheingau | Germany | 1745 |
| Auxerre | France | 1845 |
| Kyneton | Vic. Aust | 1874 |
| Blenheim | New Zealand | 2050 |
| Coonawarra | South Aust | 2200 |
| Gisborne | New Zealand | 2315 |
| Napa | California | 2400 |
| Burgundy | France | 2400 |
| Geneva-Erie | New York | 2400 |
| North East | Pennsylvania | 2450 |

## REGION TWO

| | | |
|---|---|---|
| Coldstream | Vic. Aust | 2500 |
| Mt Barker | West Aust | 2597 |
| Paw Paw | Michigan | 2600 |
| Bordeaux | France | 2632 |
| Marg. River | West Aust | 2950 |
| Asti | Italy | 2980 |

## REGION THREE

| | | |
|---|---|---|
| Egg Harbor | New Jersey | 3000 |
| Bendigo | Vic. Aust | 3081 |
| Clare | South Aust | 3235 |
| Livermore | California | 3260 |
| Adelaide | South Aust | 3458 |
| Rutherglen | Vic. Aust | 3490 |

## REGION FOUR

| | | |
|---|---|---|
| Middleburg | Virginia | 3500 |
| Baltimore | Maryland | 3500 |
| Florence | Italy | 3530 |
| Cincinnati | Ohio | 3600 |
| Duoro Valley | Portugal | 3765 |
| Augusta | Missouri | 3800 |
| Berri | South Aust | 3840 |
| Swan Valley | West Aust | 3859 |

## REGION FIVE

| | | |
|---|---|---|
| Mildura | Vic. Aust | 4073 |
| Pokolbin | NSW Aust | 4072 |
| Griffith | NSW Aust | 4100 |
| Edenton | North Carolina | 4600 |
| Altus | Arkansas | 5000 |
| Atlanta | Georgia | 5100 |
| Algiers | Algeria | 5200 |

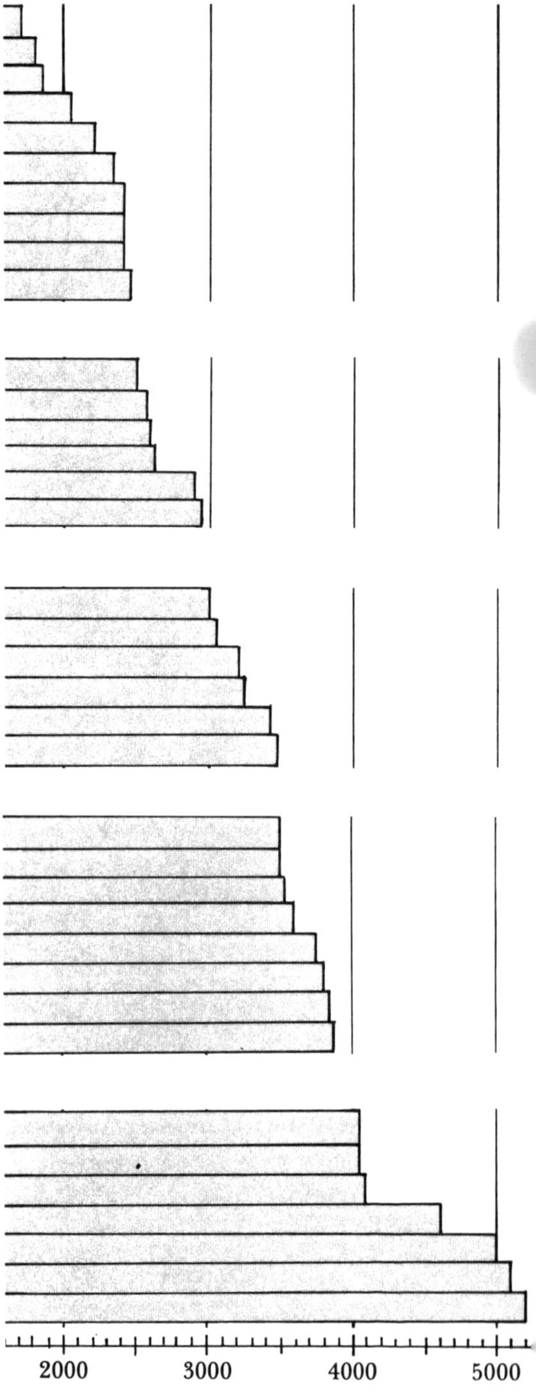

*Wine No 4:* A badly made wine using poor quality grapes.

WINE FOUR

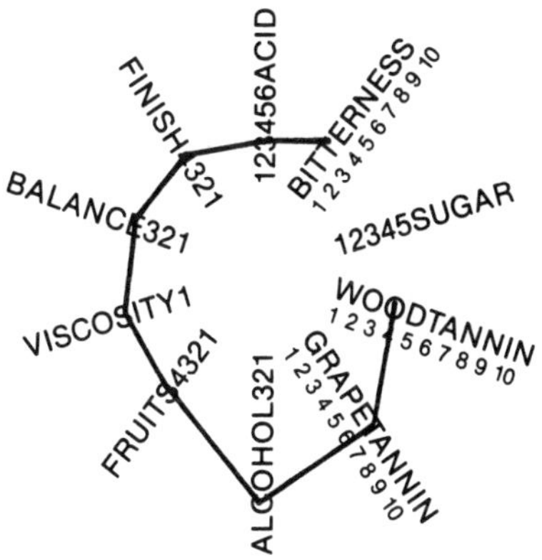


By carefully recording your impressions on the profiles we are able, at a glance, to tell why these wines are different, even though they were made from the same variety. This a good method to highlight the differing vinification methods within one appellation.

## WINE EVALUATION RECORD

INTERNATIONAL WINE ACADEMY

Occasion ______________________

Place ______________ Date ______________

| | WINE | PRICE | SIGHT 4 MAX | AROMA/ BOUQUET 6 MAX | IN MOUTH 6 MAX | AFTER-TASTE 3 MAX | OVERALL 2 MAX | TOTAL 20 MAX |
|---|---|---|---|---|---|---|---|---|
| 1 | | | | | | | | |
| 2 | | | | | | | | |
| 3 | | | | | | | | |
| 4 | | | | | | | | |
| 5 | | | | | | | | |
| 6 | | | | | | | | |

| FOOD PAIRING |
|---|
| |
| |
| |
| |
| |
| |

## PRIOR TO TASTING

| | |
|---|---|
| *1. Sight* | |
| Appearance: | Brilliant, star-bright, bright, clear, dule, cloudy, precipitated. |
| Colour: | Colourless, very light/light/straw, straw green, light/medium/dark gold. |
| | Pink, rose, light/purplish/medium/dark/tawny/brick red. |
| Saturation: | Light, medium, deep. |
| Bubbles: | Spritzig, size, quantity, rate, duration. |
| *2. Olfactory* | |
| Aroma: | Fruity, floral, spicey, vegetative, earthy. |
| Bouquet: | Clean, fresh, dirty ($H_2S$, mercaptans, etc), yeasty, oak, $SO_2$, alcohol (no irritation). |
| Intensity: | $SO_2$, alcohol (irritating). |

## IN MOUTH

| | |
|---|---|
| *3. Gustatory* | |
| Viscosity: | Watery, thin, medium, full-bodied. |
| Taste: | Sugar/sweet, bitter, sour. |
| Olfactory/flavour: | Earthy, fruity, floral herbaceous, woody, sweet, complex. |
| Tactile: | Temperature, texture, irritation, gas. |

# GUIDE TO SCORING

## IN MOUTH

| | | |
|---|---|---|
| 6 points | Extraordinary | Unmistakable characteristic aroma of grape variety or wine type. Extraordinary balance. Smooth, full bodied, mouth filling and overwhelming. |
| 5 points | Excellent | All of the above but a little less. Excellent but not overwhelming. |
| 4 points | Good | Characteristic grape variety or wine type flavour. Good balance. Smooth. May have minor faults. Good wine. |
| 3 points | Pleasant | Undistinguished wine but pleasant. |
| 2 points | Acceptable | Undistinguished wine with minor imperfections and/or more pronounced faults than 5, 4 or 3 above. |
| 1 point | Poor | Offensive flavours. May be drinkable with strong foods. |
| 0 points | Objectionable | Undrinkable. |

## AFTERTASTE

| | | |
|---|---|---|
| 2 points | Excellent | Lingering outstanding aftertaste. |
| 1 point | Good | Pleasant aftertaste. |
| 0 points | Poor | Little or no distinguishable aftertaste. |

## OVERALL

| | |
|---|---|
| 2 points | Excellent |
| 1 point | Good |
| 0 points | Poor |

# A SUMMARY OF TASTE

1. The sense of taste is a very limited sense that covers only the perception of sugar, sour, salt and bitter. Each individual has a different threshold for these components.
2. The senses of taste, touch and smell make up the overall flavour impression. Until you learn to distinguish the difference between these three senses, there is little point in proceeding further.
3. When we have a common cold we lose our sense of smell, taste is rarely affected.
4. Our taste buds are replaced at about weekly intervals.
5. There are no general groupings for the basic taste sensations of acid (sour), sugar, salt. These can be perceived with equal sensitivity all over the mouth. However, it does vary from one individual to another. Bitterness is most pronounced at the rear of the mouth.
6. Acid gives wine life and freshness, sugar contributes to viscosity. Wines with high acidity and low pH are likely to be better cellaring wines, consistent with the other factors of flavour being present.
7. Learn to discriminate the difference between sugar and sweet.
8. Bitterness and astringency, in detectable quantities, are essential components of taste and flavour in young red wines.

## LIQUID CHROMATOGRAPHY CHART

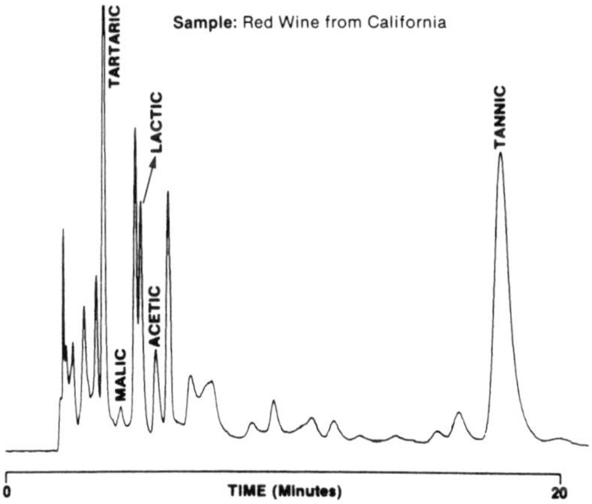


# SOME TASTY WORDS

*Oral Cavity:* The mouth.
*Overall Flavour impression:* A combination of the smell, touch and taste sense.
*Papillae:* The rough surface of the tongue that contains the taste buds.
*Physiology:* The science of essential life processes.
*Sapid:* Substances that have taste.
*Threshold:* The intensity below which a stimulus cannot be perceived and can produce no response.
*Vegemite/Marmite:* Australian vegetable extract spread. Used mainly for spreading on toast at breakfast or children's sandwiches.
*Volatile Acids:* Acids that are steam distillable acetic, butyric, formic, and propionic.

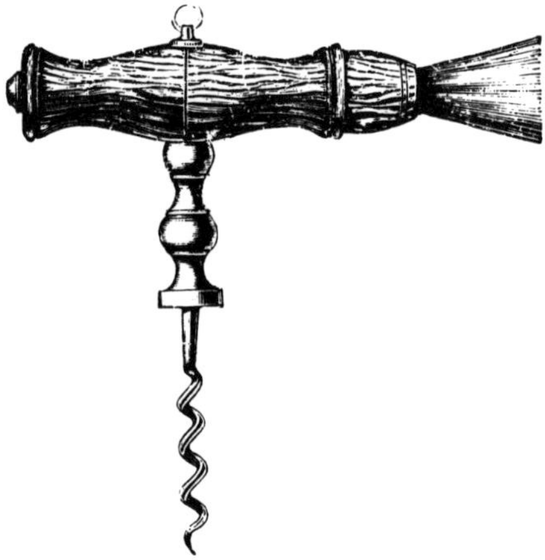

# TOUCH – TACTILE

Either we want to live or we want to die, and while we are alive
surely want to live more abundantly, to fulfil our potential,
to realise our capacities, instead of living a death of a life.
We cannot be fully alive if our feelings are dead.
R.D. Laing

# THE TACTILE SENSE

The dictionary gives us a simplistic definition of the tactile sense: 'of, perceived by, connected with the sense of touch'.

Food scientists and researchers have wrestled with the definition of just the texture part of the tactile sense for many years and still agree to disagree. Up to this time there is no single definition of texture, which plays a major role in the evaluation of both food and beverages.. Jowett (1974) offers this definition of texture: 'The attribute of a substance resulting from a combination of physical properties and perceived by the senses of touch (including kinesthesis and mouthfeel), sight and hearing. Physical properties may include size, shape, number, nature and conformation of constituent structural elements.'

So, it's not so simple! This is the nature of the problem we face when trying to make useful judgements of wine or food; we know so little about our senses, yet there are so many wine and food experts. Unfortunately, the international wine industry has been so involved in the numbers game about the amounts of acid, sugar and alcohol which instruments can measure, that many other important issues such as flavour have been overlooked. A small number of forward looking wineries and research institutes are the rare exceptions.

When we use such common wine descriptions as bubbly, sparkling, creamy, light/full body, rough, smooth, round, velvety, coarse, thin, hot, peppery, to list a few, we are referring not to the taste but rather the tactile sense and mainly to the texture aspect of that sense.

## PHYSIOLOGY OF TOUCH

The skin of our body contains many different nerve endings – the two general classes of receptors that interest us in food and beverage evaluation are the mechano-receptors for tactile sensations and the chemo-receptors for food chemicals discussed in relation to smell and taste. The mechano-receptors allow us to perceive a dozen or more touch sensations. Nearest the surface of the skin are the free nerve endings that register pain, coldness and continuous touch. A little deeper are touch and pressure receptors, deeper still are the heat receptors and nerve endings that monitor movement affecting the hair follicles.

All sensory information goes to the egg shaped thalamus in the middle of the brain. The thalamus, a type of clearing house, sorts information and directs it to the cortex (surface of the brain). Different parts of the cortex receive information from each set of sense organs; these areas cover the brain like segments of an orange - the segments are proportionate to the importance of the sense. Smell and taste areas are small, but touch covers a wide band across the brain where sensitive parts of our body such as the hands and the lips take up a large part of the cortex.

The sensitivity of the skin varies in different parts of the body – high sensitivity on the tip of the tongue, lips and tips of the fingers (as any good lover knows) – low sensitivity on the back of the hands. The back of the knee has many more pain receptors than the tip of the nose. As with our other senses – sight, hearing, smell – we all have a personal threshold for each touch sense. Our body will monitor the environment in which we live, be it Alaska or Algeria, and adjust our thermal requirements; sports persons and soliders learn to absorb high levels of pain, while surgeons, masseurs, artists and the like, learn the art of delicate touch.

## THE ORAL CAVITY, OR THE MOUTH

Following the sight and smell appraisals, the mouth becomes the wine evaluator's principal tool-of-trade. One of the 'hand-me-downs' from the past that always fascinates me is the use of the word 'palate' – 'he/she has a good palate'. Anatomically we have a soft palate at the rear of the mouth, and a hard palate joining the soft palate to the teeth. My fascination is that the palate, particularly the hard palate, has little to do with our ability to perceive or discriminate the sense of taste. It's for this reason, in this work, that there are references to the oral cavity, starting with the lips, gums, teeth (rarely mentioned in references to perception), cheeks, tongue and throat. However, the roof of the mouth has an important role in both touch and mechanical senses.

So, what is the palate? Did 'palatability' come from the palate or vice versa? My dictionary isn't very helpful.

As noted in the Olfaction chapter (Physiology of Smell), during wine appraisal, a sense similar to touch starts with the act of smelling when we are able to perceive high levels of $SO_2$ and alcohol as irritants. While it is thought that these vapours do stimulate the free nerve endings of the trigeminal nerves, they are perceived as irritants or pain rather than smell and, as such, could be considered as feel or touch sensations. (A popular theory accepts that these vapours which irritate the eyes, nose or mouth have no relation at all with touch, taste or smell.)

When I poll winelovers around the world regarding the importance of the various senses in food and beverage evaluation, touch is rarely mentioned. (No city or nation has any monopoly in this area.) Yet, after smell, touch must vie with colour as the next most important sense. Why then is touch more important than taste? Erroneously, taste has historically been associated with touch and flavour, and only in recent times have these terms been rightfully separated. If we are fully to understand the true nature of our senses and the part they play in evaluation, we must be definitive about these terms and their roles. As with colour, the importance of the tactile sense has never been stressed (to my knowledge) and I can only put this down to the fact that we know so little about the subject.

Secondly, the tactile sense gives us the mouth feel in food and beverages and covers our responses to the salient points of:

1. Temperature – hot, warm, cold.
2. Pain and irritation – burning, itching, pricking, aching, sharp pain.
3. Pressure: light touch – as a mosquito on your nose; firm touch – as in sitting down.
4. Vibration – gas in wine, also rough and smooth.
5. Spatial – form/shape.

## TEMPERATURE

Let's take temperature first. It's thought that the mouth contains fewer warm receptors than the fingers – one of the reasons why we can drink hot beverages that are too hot when spilt on our body. Even so, we are able to make judgements of slight temperature variation – and temperature is, possibly, the touch sense that is paramount in our evaluation of food and beverages.

Few people enjoy cola, beer, whisky, if they are served warm or a roast dinner or hamburger that's cold. Despite the tempeature difference, they really do *taste* the same. However, they are perceived quite differently, mainly because of the lack of smell stimulus; or after being processed by the brain which has been programmed according to our cultural or family backgrounds. (A cold beer tastes better to a thirsty person on a hot day. Is the satisfaction from the coldness, flavour, taste, or the brain's program? People can live without beer and receive similar pleasure from cold water, wine, tea or fruit juices. Many people enjoy hot tea, coffee or curry on hot days.)

Coldness is a first class anaesthetic. Why then do we have whisky and other spirits 'on the rocks', ice cold cola or almost frozen beer? Is this done deliberately to kill the flavour? Such drastic temperature reduction can do nothing other than nullify the flavour and aroma of any food or beverage. Many years ago the chefs of the world realised the aroma benefits of serving hot food, so much so that nowadays we refuse food that is not piping hot, regardless of how good the flavour is! At the other extreme, beverages such as tea or coffee that are too hot are *also* tasteless.

Champagne is served cold (36-42°F) as coldness retains the bubbles in solution thus adding to the essential character of the beverage. As white wines and roses have no bubbles there is no benefit (other than loss of flavour and aroma) in chilling them to the same low temperature - or can an ice bucket be discerning? For these styles 50°F is ideal. The only exception is a wine with undesirably high amounts of $SO_2$; the coldness will reduce the volatility of this unpleasant gas. (Many faulty wines can be passed of in this manner!)

Unfortunately, the international winelover has been intimidated into believing that red wines should be served at 'room' temperature (without being told that this odd measurement of temperature approximates 65°F), and that white wines should be served at nearly freezing temperature. In warm climates I always ask for an ice bucket to cool my red wines. In cold climates I play a continual 'chess game' with wine waiters as I take near frozen bottles of white wine from the ice bucket, only to see attentive waiters return and carefully nestle it back among the frozen chips – 'your move next'.

During seminars in many countries I have introduced a pair of identical wines – one served chilled, the other warm. The warmer wine appears to be fuller bodied (more viscous) and sweeter while the colder wine is perceived as more acid and less viscous i.e. thinner/lighter. Also, the colder wine will be far less volatile and any bitterness will be less obvious.

A good example of this was quoted in the Akron *Beacon Journal* by Katherine Brewster after she attended one of my seminars in Cleveland, Ohio. 'Young even plays dirty tricks to hammer home the notion that wines are best evaluated when served at the proper temperatures. Participants are asked to judge two white wines. Discussion provokes vast differences in what turns out to be two identical wines served in extreme opposite temperature conditions.' Now, this seminar wasn't a group of new chums, rather a group of winemakers, importers and generally well informed people. How could this happen? Easily, and does everyday to the unsuspecting and untrained.

## PAIN – IRRITATION

These are important factors in our food and beverage assessment. Indians love hot curries, far hotter than the capacity of most Caucasians. Hot chillies are enjoyed throughout the Spanish speaking world and the cultures of the Far East.

Only in recent times, 1985, has the 'hot' component of chilli been identified as capsaiacin. This also brought into prominence another sensory system, the poly-monol-nocice, which responds to both chemical and hot temperature stimulation. Pepper steaks and black pepper dishes are becoming increasingly popular in the western cuisine; obviously an acceptable level of irritation from peppers, curry, mustard and other spices can be pleasant flavour sensations. The pepper character (as opposed to the hot/peppery sensation of high alcohol wine) can be perceived in both the smell and 'mouth-feel' of particular red wines, notably zinfandel and syrah from cool growing regions.

Pain and irritation sensations in beverages are generated by a number of wine components:

1. Alcohol. Above 12 per cent by volume, alcohol impinges on the pain receptors in the bottom of the nasal cavity. Higher levels of alcohol in wine can also irritate the eyes.

2. Sulphur dioxide ($SO_2$) is the one component used from the time the grapes are picked until the finished wine is bottled. In correct proportions (20-100 ppm, with the exception of the sweet white sauternes styles where the amount ranges 150-200 ppm) $SO_2$ is an important stablising agent used for anti-bacterial purposes and as an oxidant inhibitor. Above 175 ppm $SO_2$ becomes a negative factor evidenced by a burnt match smell that impinges on the free nerve endings inside the top of the nose during the smell appraisal, plus leaving a drying condition in the mount (particularly during the aftertaste) that is most noticeable on the roof of the mouth.

$SO_2$ is expressed as bound, free and total sulphur. Bound sulphur is that chemically bound to compounds such as the carbonyls which include acetaldehyde. Sulphur dioxide also binds to sugars. Free sulphur, as the name suggests, is unbound and able to be volatilised (freed from the wine). Surprisingly, total sulphur (unlike acids) is the combination of bound and free sulphur.

If you have a wine exhibiting excessive sulphur, try pouring it from one container to another – back and forth several times – the more splashing the better. This will allow the gas to escape and the wine will be far more pleasant, if ever so slightly oxidised. Just simply allowing the wine to sit in the glass or carafe will help the sulphur volatilise.

## PRESSURE

This is the form – the shape and weight – of the food or beverage in the mouth. The main components affecting pressure in wine are:

1. Grape tannin.
2. Wood tannin.
3. Viscosity – a combination of sugar, alcohol and the polymers.

Fortified wines containing higher alcohol (and particularly those with sugar) exert more pressure on the nerve endings and give us the feeling of viscosity. The contributing components of viscosity/body are: sugar – discussed in the taste chapter; alcohol – discussed above; glycerol – a colourless, odourless, viscous liquid which is very sweet and obtained as a by product of grape sugar fermentation. (Also used in the manufacture of explosives, cellulose films, synthetic resins and many other products).

## ALCOHOL

The main alcohol resulting from the fermentation of the grape sugars, fructose and glucose, is ethyl alcohol (ethanol). Other alcohols with longer carbon chains exist in small amounts and play an important role in the aroma, flavour and general form of the wine. Ethanol gives wine body or viscosity. Table wines with low ethanol content have a 'thin' (low viscosity) character and those with too high concentrations can be flat and 'hot'. (If the lady's orange or tomato juice has a hot spot in the middle of the tongue – beware! Someone has added a healthy slug of alcohol.)

Like any other anaesthesia, the first action of ethyl alcohol is on the highest centers of the brain, with emotions, inhibitions, judgement and mental clarity being affected. Further amounts increasingly affect the central nervous system, decreasing muscular coordination, perception and reaction time. (This is the basic problem with drinking alcohol and driving.)

Alcohol can irritate the eyes to the extent that when smelling some high alcohol wines your eyes will actually weep. Alcohol normally registers as warmth in the center of the tongue; high alcohol wines are 'hot' (and maybe peppery) all over the mouth, causing pain or irritation and leaving a 'drying' sensation. This hot sensation can be greatly increased by the combination of ethanol and the bitter substance quinine sulphate.

## ALCOHOL LEVELS

The normal alcohol levels of popular wine styles are:

- White, rose and red table wines: 10-14 per cent by volume, some German white table wines as little as 7 per cent; some Californian red and white table wines are higher in alcohol.
  Sherry, port, vermouth, marsala and flavoured wines: 17-21 per cent by volume.

The aroma, touch and taste perception of alcohol, more particularly in the fortified wines, depends largely on the wine style. Wines containing high sugar levels (such as port and the sweeter sherries) tend to have even the harshest alcohol masked; while styles such as the drier sherries, say fino, without the sugar mask but with high levels of both alcohol and aldehydes, can be moderately painful.

## ALCOHOL EXERCISE

Make up an alcohol water solution by adding a dessertspoon of vodka to three ounces of water. Note the smoothness and fullness of body/viscosity plus the warm spot in the middle of the tongue – this will probably be accompanied by a persistent irritation or overall warmth in the mouth during the aftertaste. If more than 12 per cent by volume when smelt, you will notice irritation in the lower part of the nose; sometimes this takes a minute or so to register.

If you receive no response from the alcohol and water mix, keep adding vodka by half teaspoon measures until you are able to perceive the irritation and heat sensations. Also note the further contributions to viscosity and sweetness. Next time you're near the brandy bottle, pour a shot into a glass, swirl it around and take a sniff. It will most probably go close to lifting off your head, because of the almost 80 per cent proof alcohol (40 per cent by vol). Now, dilute this with an equal amount of water and take another sniff – you should be able to pick up all sorts of nuances because you're not being assaulted by the spirit. Maybe there is a sniff of the original wine, maybe the vanillin of oak. Brandy has a complexity of flavours and aromas if you can quell the alcohol. Of course, these subtleties are all lost when we have spirits 'on the rocks', try it!

One problem of evaluating a number of high alcohol wines can be that the alcohol enters the bloodstream through the oral cavity mucous membranes. Yes, you can get 'high' without swallowing a drop!

## ALCOHOL RECORD CHART

Record your perception of these components on a scale of 10

| | | WEAK 1 2 3 | MODERATE 4 5 6 7 | STRONG 8 9 10 |
|---|---|---|---|---|
| Teeth | Upper | . . . | . . . . | . . . |
| | Lower | . . . | . . . . | . . . |
| Gums | Upper | . . . | . . . . | . . . |
| | Lower | . . . | . . . . | . . . |
| Lips | Upper | . . . | . . . . | . . . |
| | Lower | . . . | . . . . | . . . |
| Tongue | Tip | . . . | . . . . | . . . |
| | Top | . . . | . . . . | . . . |
| | Sides | . . . | . . . . | . . . |
| Cheeks | Front | . . . | . . . . | . . . |
| | Rear | . . . | . . . . | . . . |
| Throat | | . . . | . . . . | . . . |
| Roof of mouth | | . . . | . . . . | . . . |

## ALCOHOL WORDS

| NEGATIVE – Too Little | | POSITIVE | NEGATIVE – Too Much |
|---|---|---|---|
| Thin | | Warm | Coarse |
| Watery | | Round | Hot |
| | | Balanced | Drying |
| | ← | Peppery | → |

## ASTRINGENCY

As mentioned in the bitterness section, bitterness and astringency go hand in hand despite bitterness being a true taste sensation, while astringency stimulates the touch sense.

Although we don't have high tolerances for bitterness or astringency several of our most popular beverages are moderately high in phenolic substances, the providers for both sensations. Here's a run down on the polyphenols in these favoured beverages: coffee heads the list with 2000 parts per million, tea next with 1600 ppm, red win has 1300 ppm, European beer about 150 ppm and American beer about half the European figure. Vanilla, cinnamon and spicy substances are some of the other flavour benefits originating from grape phenolics. But, as tannins provide much of wine's sensory character we'll deal with that here. As mentioned in the colour chapter, wine's colour pigments are also phenolic substances.

Wine has grape and wood tannins, both with similar touch sensations; my experience is that we perceive them in different parts of the mouth. Grape tannin is more likely to be noticable on the teeth, lips and front of the cheeks as a rough 'furry' sensation; wood tannin is more of a warm sensation on the insides of the cheeks, further to the rear. Grape tannin is bitter and high levels can cause mild pain by acting on the free nerve endings. 'Grip' is a word associated with the mouth feel of grape tannin, particularly in the aftertaste. This gripping sensation can be so assertive that you think that your teeth are being drawn out through your ears! (This is gripping!)

Grape tannin is often called the 'backbone' or 'spine' of the wine and one favourable factor about aggressively tannic and/or astringent wines is that, provided they are combined with a commensurate amount of fruit and acid, they will have the potential for a long cellaring life. It can be assumed that a degree of grape tannin is a measure of the wine's ability to age gracefully. In young wines this tannin can be unattractive; it's best that we don't always rush our reds. Your trusted wine merchant can provide you with advice and examples here.

Diacetyl is the love/hate by product of malolactic fermentation. At levels below 1.5 ppm it plays out its love role in subduing phenolic and related bitterness in red wines, and in some of the 'bigger' Californian chardonnays. It does this by smoothing the mouth feel, thus lightening the touch on the pressure receptors and relieving the astringency feeling. Diacetyl is identified by its 'butter' smell – in fact, it is added to margarine to make it smell like butter. In everyday use, diacetyl is found in cheese, adding that buttery smell, especially to cheddars. In beer it also provides a butter smell, where it can also contribute to sourness.

### ASTRINGENCY EXERCISES

To learn more about the mouth feel of astringency, go to your local pharmacist and obtain a pinch of alum. Add this to an ounce of water and roll this mix around your mouth. If you do this, I'll give you a guarantee that you'll not quickly forget what astringency is, and forever be able to differentiate between astringency and bitterness.

For the tannin mix, you'll need to obtain some grape tannin from your local home winemaker supply store, mix this with a little vodka or ethanol and add to wine rather than water. A large pinch should be sufficient for a one to two ounce wine sample, preferably red. Having something pleasant to rinse your mouth or drink after doing both these mixes – they are not likely to be among your great taste sensations, but certainly a great learning experience.

### VIBRATION – GAS – CARBON DIOXIDE IN WINE

Most people are familiar with the importance of the $CO_2$ component in sparkling wines (it gives them the sparkle!), gas can be noticed in many white wines, and, indeed some red wines, both by design and as a curse. The bubbles that appear in white table wines and can be seen adhering to the bottom sides of the glass are known as 'spritzig' (German) or French – 'petillant'. They are a product of bottling procedures and indicate that the wine has been carefully handled at that time but in no way reflects on the quality of the wine.

## A TOUCHING SUMMARY

1. The touch sense, in all its forms, is the least understood when it comes to the evaluation of food or beverages.

2. This sense covers the important factors of vibration – rough, smooth, sparkling; texture; viscosity or body; temperature – cold, warm, hot; hot as in peppery, alcoholic.

3. We can quickly improve our evaluation skills if we learn to differentiate between the touch and taste senses, and then learn to verbalise these differences. Practise the words with the exercises.

4. Remember, there are two palates, soft and hard, each with its own role. Be ever vigilant about registrations all over the mouth, including the lips, gums, teeth, roof of the mouth and throat area.

5. Be alert to the significance of irritation of the eyes, nose and mouth.

6. Nothing fools the wine judge more than temperature, cold or warm wine.

7. Room temperature is ideal for red table wines, but room temperature is between 65-70°F (18-20°C), not a tent in the Sahara or an igloo in Iceland.

8. Work hard at learning the difference between astringency and bitterness; also grape and wood tannins. Use the exercises provided.

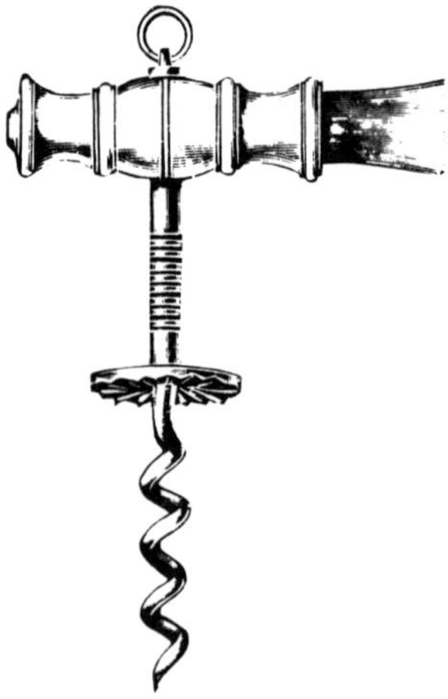

# THE HUMAN BRAIN

No matter how much we learn about the brain we can never learn it all. There will always be something to astound us, to amaze us, to keep us humble, while at the same time stimulating us to greater efforts toward understanding the brain. The human brain is simply the most marvellous organ in the known universe.

DR MILES HERKENTHAM, NATIONAL INSTITUTE OF MENTAL HEALTH, USA

The essence of this chapter – *The Human Brain* – originally appeared in the 1981 Annual Report of International Flavours and Fragrances Inc., and set new standards for work in this field. For the layman, in the first instance, it might be heavy going – skip it if you like. However, the more we understand about the workings of the brain, the more we will understand how our body works – and particularly our senses and the part they play in the enjoyment of the essential nuances of food and beverages.

# THE HUMAN BRAIN

The brain is the source of all our dreams, our moods, our thoughts, our actions. The brain is three pounds or more of tens of billions of nerve cells (neurons) and many more billions of glial (supporting) cells. Its ceaseless day and night activity needs massive amounts of oxygen and calories, derived mainly from glucose. These, as well as other necessities such as amino acids, ions and hormones, are transported or diffused across the protective blood-brain-barrier into the brain.

The complexity of the inter-connections of these billions of nerve cells and their ability to process information defies the imagination. It is estimated that some of them may have ten thousand or more connections with other neurons.

## THE HYPOTHESIS

Brain input from smell and taste (the chemical senses) receptors are now known to affect not only olfaction (smell) and gustation (taste) but also behaviour, memory and learning, various emotional states and possibly other activities essential to both mental and physical wellbeing.

It seems reasonable to postulate, therefore, that in the next decade further advances of the neurosciences will clarify not only the way the brain handles information coming from the chemical senses but also their role, along with that of nutrition, in the normal functioning of the brain and in the prevention and treatment of disturbed mental function.

## NEURAL COMMUNICATION

The largest number of neurons is found in the central nervous system – the spinal cord and the brain. The peripheral nervous system, including its autonomic (a number of the body's selfgoverning systems) components, extends a network of nerve fibres over the entire body.

Neurons communicate with each other by a combination of electrical and chemical signals in a complicated series of events. The message is usually carried electrically within each neuron, and chemically between neurons. The events start with an induced change of membrane followed, within a few hundred microseconds, by a reverse flow of potassium ions (an electrically charged atom) to the outside of the membrane. The nerve impulses, thus generated, travel down the length of the axon to the nerve terminal. There, a change in the electrical conductance of the terminal membrane admits calcium into the terminal.

This 'firing' releases a chemical messenger, a neurotransmitter, which diffuses across the tiny synaptic cleft (the point of contact between cells) which separates neurons. The transmitter, in turn, initiates changes in the ionic conductance of the postsynaptic membrane to produce either excitation or inhibition, in a sort of 'go' or 'no-go' manner. Actually the result is more complicated because the neuron has a mechanism for integrating the totality of the excitatory and inhibitory inputs and expressing that net sum by its own rate of discharge or 'firing'. It can do its own thing!

Human actions are ultimately the net results of decisions made by the central nervous system resulting from many input channels. The effect of inputs is presumed to differ from individual to individual. In other words, whether we cut our finger, see a great painting, hear a superb orchestra or taste an excellent glass of wine – all sensations travel to the cerebral cortex for interpretation, judgement, decisions; the reactions occur in the finger, the eye, the ear or the mouth, but only after orders (the motor signals) from the brain have returned to the point of contact.

When we cut a finger, a message flashes to the brain, the sense of pain speeds to the finger and another complex mechanism files away a message telling you not to be so stupid next time you use a sharp knife. Some people make a major performance of a cut finger, others ignore the same problem. If you think that your personal computer is really something then consider the capacity of your brain, it can store about 15 million pieces of worthwhile information and trivia.

## THE LIMBIC SYSTEM

The central olfactory (smell) pathways have traditionally been included within the rhinencephalon (the smell brain), the so-called limbic system. That system connects certain areas of the cerebral cortex (the grey matter) with other parts of the brainstem and diencephalon (a part of the forebrain) which control such autonomic and endocrine (gland which secretes hormones into the blood) functions as heart rate, blood pressure, breathing, reproductive behaviour, response to stress, etc. It is linked with the hypothalamus, a part of the brain which controls the pituitary gland and thus the release of the body's hormones. A striking example of the action of smell on the endocrine system, via the hypothalamus and the pituitary, is the reported synchronisation of the menstrual cycles of females living together, the McClintock effect.

Sight and hearing have commonly been thought to be the sense most responsible for the remarkable advances in human brain function. But since the 1930s, scientists have wondered about possible functions of the limbic system apart from its role in smell. The rhinencephalon constitutes a sizeable part of the brain in man as it has in his hominoid predecessors for several million years.

Over this evolutionary period it has been connected with the central problems of existence – hunger, danger and reproduction.

Through its connections with other brain areas the limbic system plays an important role in the integration of emotional behaviour. In man, certain parts of the system are essential for learning and memory. The anecdotal connection of odour and memory is part of everyone's personal experience. Long lost memory can be suddenly recalled through electrical stimulation by electrodes placed in the temporal lobe of patients undergoing brain surgery. A major part of the limbic system is located in the temporal lobe. Through the limbic system, smell and taste have access to neural complexes that affect much of human conscious and unconscious behaviour.

### EAU DE GENEVIEVE

In 1977 Michael Russell reported a study he had conducted at San Francsico State University. A colleague of Russell's named Genevieve was gathering information about the onset of women's menstrual cycles, and after several months she noticed something peculiar. The menstrual cycles of women with whom she had personal contact, appeared to alter so that they became more and more like her own cycle, in terms of when they began and ended. Russell wondered if olfaction could be responsible. Since some of the most potent scent glands in human beings are on the underarms, Russell had Genevieve wear cotton pads under her arms for several days in order to collect perspiration. Then he ran an experiment in which volunteer women had a substance painted on their upper lip three times a week for four months. Half the applicants received alcohol, the other half received a combination of alcohol and Genevieve's underarm perspiration. The menstrual cycles of the first group did not change, and their cycle starting dates averaged about 9.3 days apart. Incredibly, the women receiving 'eau de Genevieve' showed a startling change; within four months their menstrual cycles were all only 3.4 days apart. Apparently some substances secreted by Genevieve was influencing the menstrual cycles of the other women, and it was obviously happening through olfactory sense (*Olfactory Synchrony*, 1977). Why there should be such a secretion, and what value it may have, is not known. Russell suspects that the mystery may have something to do with oestrogen, a female hormone.

# THE CHEMICAL SENSES

### OLFACTION (SMELL)

Our knowledge of the mechanism of olfaction is far from complete. Some of the most important odour information processing takes place within the mucous layer of the olfactory epithelium at the top of the nasal cavity. Odour molecules link to specialised receptor sites (lock and key molecules – see olfactory chapter) on the membranes of the hairlike cilia attached to the millions of olfactory neurons found there. It is not yet known whether there are specific receptors for specific odours, but we do know that olfactory receptors can monitor the environment with great precision. Humans, as well as many other animals, can distinguish odour due to quite small variations in the chemical structures of the odour molecule.

The central parts of the olfactory nerves enter the two olfactory bulbs which are immediately behind the nose, one on either side of the midline of the brain. The anatomy and chemistry of the bulbs are distinctive and in several ways unlike most other brain regions.

Presumably, chemical substances which modify or block the action of neurotransmitters found in the bulbs would have major effects upon the olfactory process. As an example, since the bulbs are rich in opiate binding sites, substances which alter binding to these sites could conceivably alter olfactory perception. The application of the new molecular tools to the study of olfactory receptors may also answer fundamental questions about odour recognition and permit the development of agents within highly selective effects.

Neural signals pass from the olfactory bulbs to other parts of the limbic system and then to the cerebral neocortex. It is through these further connections that the olfactory systems affect overall brain functioning including learning and memory, sexual behaviour and regulation.

The neurotransmitters which are most highly concentrated in the limbic system include many that are known to mediate actions of the major agents that releive the symptoms of mental illness. The principal anti-schizophrenic, anti-depressant and anti-anxiety drugs are thought to owe their therapeutic effects to their influence upon the limbic system.

There may be even more direct ways in which the olfactory brain is related to emotional disorders. Olfactory hallucinations are well known in schizophrenia. Patients often complain that the major problem with their lives is that they 'stink'. Some psychiatrists and their nurses can identify some schizophrenics by a characteristic odour. The possibility of utilising odourants in the therapy of schizophrenia is under investigation.

Scientists usually solve complicated problems by investigating relatively simple systems that can be models for complex ones. The olfactory system may provide a relatively simple model for the study of more general brain functions; that is in the future.

## TASTE – GUSTATION

Our knowledge of the mechanism of gustation is greater than that of olfaction, but it is still incomplete. The common perception of flavour is actually a combination of odour and taste inputs plus texture and temperature. Here we are concerned only with the four basic tastes – bitter, salt, sour and sugar.

Taste and smell interact closely in determining our appreciation of food. Early man utilised the sense of taste to monitor poisons, which were often bitter, from calorically valuable foods which tended to be sweet. Taste is important for modern man as well. Many diseases, medications and other therapies interefere with our ability to taste. Many of those so affected lose any interest in eating. Frequently they develop psychiatric disturbances in addition to physical deterioration.

Taste perception begins with specific receptor cells in the taste buds located primarily on the tongue but also on other parts of the oral cavity. While numerous, the taste receptors are far less in number than the olfactory receptors. Unlike the olfactory receptors, the taste receptors are not themselves neurons but connect with neurons whose processes lead to the brain. It is not yet clear why one can taste different flavours selectively in different portions of the tongue, sugar in the front, for example.

Some scientists believe that these traditional taste groupings will be resolved into distinctive subgroups by further research and that additional flavour will be identified.

Small variations in chemical structure can cause major alterations in taste as well as in smell. Very minor variations in the amino acid structure of peptides can transform a molecule totally from sweet to bitter. Presumably, specific receptor sites exist on the membranes of the taste cells which interact selectively with flavour molecules. And as with the olfactory system, it is likely that applying the new, powerful molecular tools of neuroscience may make it possible to isolate these taste receptors and work out the mechanism whereby we recognise and discriminate between flavours.

The taste cells communicate with neural taste firbres which in turn travel to a relay station in the brainstem, the nucleus of the solitary tract, and from there to the pons (a communication bridge), the thalamus and ultimately the cortex. The solitary tract influences much of the body's internal environment such as blood pressure regulation and vomiting. This is almost certainly why extremely bad tasting food makes us nauseous – presumably to protect us from poisons. Similarly, a fall in blood pressure can make us feel faint and nauseous.

## BRAIN SUMMARY

A stimulus is any chemical or physical activator which initiates a response in a sense receptor. There are several classes of stimuli that interest the wine-lover at work. These are: 1. mechanical, 2. thermal, 3. chemical.

An effective stimulus produces a sensation, the dimensions of which are: quality, intensity, duration, like and dislike (hedonic).

The stimuli, in each class, are measured by physical or chemical methods; the sensation by psychological procedures. The least energy capable of producing a sensation is called the 'detection threshold'. As the stimulus energy is increased, sensations change in lawful ways which are slightly different for each sense. The least stimulus change perceptible is termed a 'difference threshold'. Both detection and difference thresholds are important concepts for gauging the relation between stimulus and sensation, a psycho-physical relationship.

For the appreciation of art we use our eyes alone, for sound we use hearing only, we use both for the appreciation of movies or television. When we place food or beverages in our mouth we use every sense except sight. Hearing is vital for the enjoyment of crackers, celery and carrots; the sense of touch is necessary to measure texture, shape and temperature, the senses of smell and taste play their obvious roles of telling us whether to accept or reject, like or dislike, what is in our mouth.

The properties in food and beverages that irritate, touch, taste, smell and sound are known as organoleptic. You may hear among the food and wine professionals the term organoleptic evaluation or appraisal; don't be alarmed that some strange disease has hit town. It simply means using our senses, rather than machines or instruments, to make judgments of food and beverages.

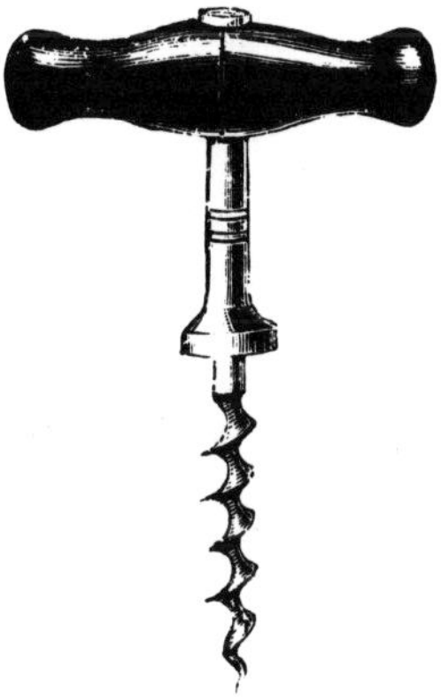

# GLASSWARE

What glassware should be used for wine appraisal?

## SHAPE AND COLOUR

If you have a set of those ornate purple, blue or green glasses that a friend gave you for a wedding present, rush out right now and smash them; take the saucer shaped 'champagne' glasses with you and give them a smashing time also. (If you have a favourite aunt who doesn't approve of waste, make a big hit by presenting them to her; they are no use for wine evaluation or enjoyment.) Coloured glasses are nothing more than a European fad to hide the oxidised colour of pour quality wine and the Hollywood-promoted champagne saucers are useful only for seaford cocktails or chocolate mousse.

Visually, wine is all about beautiful colours – purples, blues, reds of a fine red wine and brilliant straw to golden colours of a white wine. Only clear glass will reveal this beauty – expensive cut glass adds nothing and as a general rule bulky glasses are poorly balanced. An additional interesting point is that not only are cut lead crystal glasses bulky and heavy, but it is also possible that they are unhealthy.

Customs authorities in most countries enforce health regulations on imported goods. In some countries infra-red lighting is used to detect the lead content of crystal glassware and bone china. Samples are rejected depending on the intensity of blue colouring that shows in the glass or china while under the light.

In these days of no asbestos, lead-free fuel, salt-free foods and non-usage of many other products once considered normal or standard, one might ponder *any* benefits of using lead crystal glasses.

The 'feel' of a glass can make people comfortable or otherwise at a meal. And those funny looking V or icrcream cone shaped martini glasses are worthless for anything other than martinis. A wineglass should taper in at the top – not taper outwards.

What's the answer?

There is every reason to believe big glasses make for better visual and olfactory appraisal. Small glasses limit the full scope of appraisal and under *no* conditions should nonglassware be considered for dining or serious evaluation; but they are certainly fine for picnic quaffing.

## FLUTES

The reasons I find the champagne flute ideal:

1. The size of an object is the most generally accepted factor in seeing. Which is the easiest to see and discriminate – F or F?
2. The flute allows for a long 'tongue' when the glass is tilted forward bringing the wine to the very rim of the glass. (What to expect in the 'tongue' is fully covered in the colour chapter.)
3. The larger the surface area of glass the better for olfactory appraisal. The volume of odour available for olfactory appraisal is directly related to the surface area of the glass wetted by wine.

## SPARKLING CLEAN

Whatever glass you choose, sparkling cleanliness is the keynote. Wherever possible, avoid the use of detergents in glass washing as this causes a film on the glass. This is disastrous for sparkling wines which just won't bubble.

On one occasion we were setting up for a dinner at which the principal guest was the New Zealand Prime Minister and, on testing the champagne flutes, we found that the wine wouldn't sparkle in the glasses. This necessitated the quick purchase, on Saturday afternoon, of some very fine wet and dry sandpaper and by rotating this in the glasses we were able to remove the residual detergent and return the glasses to a useful state.

Make sure that your white wines aren't so cold that they frost up the outside the glass. Condensation is hard to see through, somewhat similar to looking through opaque glass, and this will have a marked effect on your ability to distinguish between brilliant, bright and clear.

Whatever glass you decide on, do not fill more than from a quarter to a third; the worst thing for evaluation is too much wine in fthe glass.

## USELESS GLASSES

## OK GLASSES

# GOOD GLASSES

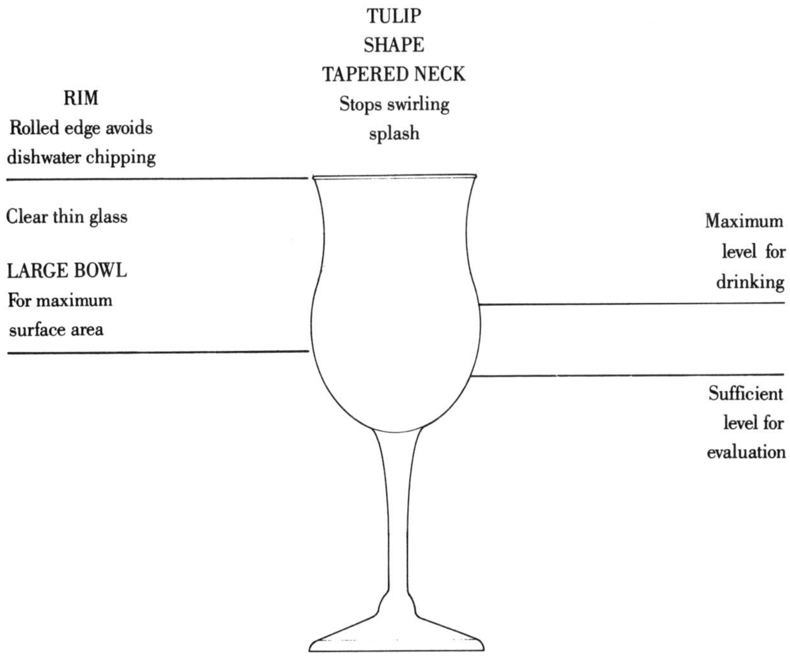

# SENSORY EVALUATION
## THE EVENT

At a much publicised chardonnay tasting conducted by Decanter Magazine in London, the distinguished panel was asked, 'What constitutes a good chardonnay?'. The replies were interesting and honest, to say the least.

Reply One: *I have no idea what constitutes a good chardonnay! It would be totally wrong to choose one style, the style we were brought up on, and say that is the right style.*

Reply Two: *Probably every taster here, and probably every person who likes chardonnay has their own idea of what constitutes a good chardonnay.*

Reply Three: *I tend to judge wines as a Frenchman, taking chardonnay to be at its best in the Cote d'Or.*

Londoners pride themselves on their wine knowledge and tasting ability – and these judges were one of the most high powered groups available. Notwithstanding these high qualifications, they entered into an evaluation with each person looking in a different direction.

## THE AIM

The moral of the story is simply this; when you are conducting, or involved in, a competition, evaluation, tasting event, call it what you will, the first criterion is to ensure that each person has a crystal clear idea of what the event hopes to achieve. Evaluations can be for a number of reasons, the most popular being hedonic, the likes or dislikes of individuals or groups. This is normally done using a scoresheet with a 20 point scale similar to those noted on page 118 and 119. By totalling the individual scores the group arrives at a ranking order, and 95 per cent of the people go away happy.

However, food and beverage professionals ignore the hedonic approach and usually work to a ranking system, using far more comprehensive scoresheets. Ranking by merit is not easy. Often it is difficult, and even a little unfair, to rank one wine above another when they might have differing favourable qualities. This brings about a trade off situation which I don't like – but decisions must be made; somebody has to win, somebody lose.

Batch quality control is used by wholesalers, distributors, hotels, restaurants and wine regions (appellations) to determine whether a particular product, be it wine or food, is relevant to the style and meets the minimum standards of that particular establishment or institution. This type of evaluation is usually made by a small group of professionals using a simple scoring system designed for that purpose, not dissimilar to the methods used for appellation control.

As mentioned in the Austrian system, the wines being presented can be judged against a wine that has previously been accepted.

## THE PLACE

Having clearly determined the aims of your event, the next requirement is a suitable room. This is never easy as there are so many factors to consider when making the choice. Foremost among these considerations are noise, colour, light, temperature and odour.

Many of the functions I attend are conducted in hotels, restaurants or rented rooms which means there is often little choice. When there is, the most isolated and quiet room is the best; choose rooms that are removed from the traffic flow and avoid adjoining rooms with a loud rock band. (Be wary of this not irregular occurrence!)

Talking is not permitted at many serious events; I do not agree with this, but any necessary speech should be kept at a quiet level. The effect of noise during an evaluation session is best described by one in a series conducted in France. When a buzzer in the room was sounded, some of the judges commenced to perspire – even though the room temperature was a mere 65-70°F.

## THE LIGHTING

I have described at some length in the sight-colour chapter the desirable lighting requirements. I can only say to be constantly aware of this important factor: I still believe that sight is second only to smell in importance during evaluation.

## THE ATMOSPHERE

Obviously, a pleasant temperature is desirable for judges to work in; most authorities recognise the optimum as being about 70°.

We are living in an age where strong perfumes, powerful room fresheners and disinfectants are the prevalent odours of the day, particularly in public buildings. These strong odours are counter-productive for wine and food evaluations. Large rooms are desirable; where possible have fresh air circulated throughout the room in advance, or at the least, have the room deodourised. For numerous reasons, smoking of any type should be prohibited, but respect the rights of smokers by having a smokers' room available nearby.

## PERMANENT EVALUATION ROOM

If you, or your group, intend to set up a room for evaluative purposes, the cubicle concept, rather than long tables, appears to be the ideal. Each judge should have a booth 30″-36″ wide, 24″ deep and upwards of 15″ high (90 × 60 × 38 cms) between cubicles.

Although gleaming white appears most popular in hospitals and clinics, wine is best judged in rooms with flat tinted paint, light grey for preference. Bright white paint, porcelain, marble and stainless steel are known to do nothing other than distort judgements.

## TABLE SETTING

I have discussed glassware earlier. The table should be covered with clean white cloths or placemats, the judges will require plenty of large, clean glasses, spit buckets (cuspidors!), water for rinsing glasses and mouths, and crackers or dry bread. No cheese, please. Finger smudges from the cheese dirties the bowl and rim of the glass and this is not easy to remove if you have access only to cold water.

## DURATION

Last but not least, an evaluation session for winelovers should not extend beyond one hour or include more than 12 wines. Professionals, with regular practice, are capable of longer concentration and application; no session should include more than 20 wines. Some people notice that there are flavours and odours that come and go in the glass during lengthy evaluations. More than likely they are the culprits and their senses are dulled or attuned to the style. This is not to say that a meeting can't last two to three hours – only that the concentrated evaluation period should not last more than one hour.

Perhaps many winelovers do not have much choice as to when they can attend a tasting, but the most favourable time for critical evaluation is late morning, prior to lunch (when the judges ae hungry!).

A suggested order, by styles, for evaluation is:

1. Sparkling wines – not sweet
2. White table wines – not sweet
3. Rose
4. Red table wines
5. Sweet sparkling wines
6. Sweet wine table wines
7. Dessert wines

## SIGHTERS

A normal gathering of wine judges in the USA will include restauranteurs, writers, cookery teachers, an attorney or two, a couple of winemakers, retailers and the usual few diehards. Here we have a collection of people (not at all similar to our London panel) from all types of backgrounds, assembled to make judgements on the professional winemakers' annual efforts. It's somewhat akin to a gathering of professional musicians, jazz, classical, military, rock and roll, all turning up at one place, without prior rehearsal or music, to play 'America the Beautiful' at the Presidential Inauguration. At least, the musicians are professional. Otherwise, there's no common thread, or intent.

In this hi-tech world, it's hard to believe that we still approach important wine judgements in this casual manner. Particularly if some of the judges cannot identify the smell of cherry or blackcherry and the rest can't agree on what constitutes a good chardonnay. The sad truth is that this is the norm, with two possible exceptions. The Beverage Testing Institute, Ithaca, New York, continually monitors its judges by placing two identical wines in many 'flights'. Should a judge not score the two wines within one point, his or her scores for that flight are disregarded. I understand that the San Francisco organisers also have a test for judges, before the event.

I am not suggesting that the many wonderful people, who provide their services without financial reward, don't have the skills necessary for this important task. What is suggested is that we should have all members of the group looking at the same spot on the horizon, rather than at each of the 360 degrees. I propose what are called 'sighters'; what a rifleman has on the shooting range – a practice shot at the target.

Using this system, the judges, at the start of the session, all evaluate one common wine. From this, everyone obtains a briefing and standards are set for the competition. It would be desirable for a 'sighter' to be used with each major class.

As has been previously pointed out, each individual perceives odours, good and bad, differently. This can lead to a situation where wines with common faults, such as hydrogen sulphite and ethyl mercaptans in small amounts, are seen as favourable attributes by some judges. It is a fact that many people cannot recognise faulty wines and the more often a faulty wine is tasted, the more likely is it to be accepted as a normal wine.

I also proposed that chemical 'sighters' are placed in an adjoining room, and that it is compulsory for judges to be able to identify the chemicals listed earlier in 'Odours to Learn'. It is a fundamental truism in wine appraisal that we are comparing now today's impressions with impressions memorised previously. My mind plays tricks; does yours? It would be of considerable benefit if local wine clubs undertook to make available some of these smell and taste 'sighters' before any of their important events.

## SCORING – RECORDING

Your impressions of wine can be recorded by nearly as many systems as there are government taxes – there is at least one for every man, woman and child. To reach a high standard of wine evaluation proficiency (and let me remind you that this is possible for the average winelover), particularly those striving for competition judge standard, it's imperative during your training programme that all perceptions are recorded.

Without a disciplined approach to the task very little is possible. Set out on the following pages are 'spider webs' and charts to cover most of your recording needs for aroma, touch, in-mouth, varietal definition and hedonic scoring. These systems have been well tested in the international sphere – we know they work and that they should meet your requirements.

As these are adapted from various sources, you may find that you or your group can also modify them to your personal needs; and needs do vary from group to group. Some wine clubs wish to find the best buys among jug wines or a group of a particular variety, whereas a winery may wish to discriminate chardonnay components from different vineyards.

*Some scoring systems are based on wine faults alone – don't fall for this trap! Look for good points.*

# TRANSLATED FROM THE OFFICE DE LA VIGNE ET DU VIN PARIS, FRANCE

| | | Multiplying factor for increasing defects | | | | |
|---|---|---|---|---|---|---|
| Characteristic | Weight | X0 | X1 | X4 | X9 | X16 |
| Appearance | 1 | | | | | |
| Colour | 1 | | | | | |
| Odour Intensity | 1 | | | | | |
| Odour Quality | 2 | | | | | |
| Taste Intensity | 2 | | | | | |
| Taste Quality | 3 | | | | | |
| Harmony | 2 | | | | | |

Multiplying factors: outstanding (0); very good (1); good (4); acceptable (9); unacceptable (16).

Name________________________________________ Date________________

The scorer multiplies defects – the higher the score the worse the wine! The Italian system uses a multiplying factor – but positively.

# A EUROPEAN WINE CLUB

Date__________

Wine__________

Vintage__________ Grape variety__________

Classification__________

Grower/shipper__________

| | Points | Characteristic |
|---|---|---|
| 1. Colour | | __________ |
| 2. Clarity | | __________ |
| 3. Bouquet | | __________ |
| 4. Flavour | | __________ |
| Total | | Notes: |

| | Max Points |
|---|---|
| 1. COLOUR | |
| white | |
| a) pale, overcoloured | 0 |
| b) light | 1 |
| c) typical | 2 |
| 2. CLARITY | |
| a) dull | 0 |
| b) bright | 1 |
| c) brilliant | 2 |
| 3. Bouquet | |
| a) defective | 0 |
| b) mute | 1 |
| c) clean | 2 |
| d) fragrant | 3 |
| e) fine and flowery | 4 |
| 4. Flavour | |
| a) defective | 0 |
| b) neutral | 1 - 3 |
| c) clean but thin | 4 - 5 |
| d) balanced | 6 - 9 |
| e) ripe and noble | 10 - 12 |

| Classification | Min Points |
|---|---|
| Qualitatswein b. A. | 11 |
| Kabinett | 13 |
| Spatlese | 14 |
| Auslese | 15 |
| Beerenauslese | 16 |
| Trockenbeerenauslese | 17 |

Fairly simple, everyday score card.

# SCORE CARD –
# ASSOCIZIONE ENOTECNICI ITALIANI

Wine Sample________________________________________________

| | Standard Value | Score |
|---|---|---|
| Appearance | 2 | |
| Colour | 2 | |
| Olfactory: | | |
| Finesse | 2 | |
| Intensity | 2 | |
| Freshness | 2 | |
| Gustatory: | | |
| Body | 2 | |
| Harmony | 2 | |
| Intensity | 2 | |
| Final Olfactory/Gustatory: | 3 | |
| Fidelity to Style | 3 | |
| General Impression | 3 | |

Multiplying factors: excellent (4); good (3); average (2); mediocre (1), bad (0).

| Taste | | |
|---|---|---|
| Body | 2 | ________________ |
| Harmony | 3 | ________________ |
| Intensity | 2 | ________________ |
| Final taste-odour sensation | 3 | ________________ |
| Typical | 3 | ________________ |
| General Impression | 3 | ________________ |

Name________________________________________________

Date________________________________________________

This Italian system uses a positive multiplying factor – making a possible 100 points.

# MURPHY SCORE CARD FOR DRY WHITE TABLE WINE

| Class | Wine No | |
|---|---|---|
| | Possible Score | Marks |
| COLOUR AND APPEARANCE | | |
| Approximation to colour of class | 5 | |
| Approximation to correct colour according to age | 5 | |
| Limpidity | 5 | |
| BOUQUET | | |
| Cleanliness | 8 | |
| Pleasantness of grape aroma | 8 | |
| Pleasantness of other aromas | 8 | |
| Intensity | 8 | |
| Approximation to bouquet of class | 3 | |
| TASTE AND FLAVOUR | | |
| Acidity according to age | 4 | |
| Sweetness according to class | 4 | |
| Gas according to class | 4 | |
| Body | 4 | |
| Taste satisfaction | 4 | |
| Cleanliness of flavour | 4 | |
| Pleasantness of flavour | 4 | |
| Complexity of flavour | 4 | |
| Bitterness | 4 | |
| Finish | 4 | |
| Balance | 4 | |
| Overall impression of taste and flavour | 4 | |
| Approximation to class | 2 | |
| | 100 | |

Dan Murphy, a Melbourne wine merchant, developed this 100 point system but found that most people scored between 65-85 so reverted to a 20 point system.

# CHAMPAGNE SCORE SHEET

Degustation du: Monsieur:

| Nos | Cuvee | Couleur Note s/3 | Mousse Note s/3 | Nez Note s/10 | Gout Note s/10 | Appre-iation Generale s10 | Total des Points | Classe M1 |
|---|---|---|---|---|---|---|---|---|
| | | | | | | | | |
| | | | | | | | | |
| | | | | | | | | |
| | | | | | | | | |
| | | | | | | | | |
| | | | | | | | | |

continued next page

Name

| STIMULATION PRIOR TO TASTING | IDENTIFICATION | INTENSITY | QUALITY |
|---|---|---|---|
| 1. VISUAL | | | |
| *Appearance:* cloudy, hazy, dull, clear,<br>bright, cristalline | | | |
| *Colour Nuance:* pale yellow, greenish yellow, straw<br>yellow, golden yellow, amber, brownish<br>yellow, pink, violet pink, *oeil de*<br>*perdrix* (light claret coloured), red,<br>ruby red, violet red, yellowish red *(tuile)*,<br>garnet red, brownish red | | | |
| *Intensity:* none, weak, light, rich,<br>strong, intense, pure, lively | | | |
| *Gas Release:*absence or presence: fine<br>bubbles, medium bubbles,<br>large bubbles | | | |
| *Viscosity:* water, syrupy, thick, oily | | | |
| 2. OLFACTORY | | | |
| *Complex Aromas:** fruit, flower, musk, musty,<br>oxidised | | | |
| *Particularized Aromas:** mercaptan, ethyl acetate,<br>hydrogen sulphide, sulphur<br>dioxide | | | |
| 3. GUSTATORY | | | |
| *Balanced Taste:* thin, soft, velvety or mellow,<br>harmonious, supple,<br>delicate, tender, full, fleshy | | | |
| *Or Dominant Taste:* acid, salty, sweet, bitter | | | |
| 4. OLFACTORY | | | |
| *Complex Aromas:** | | | |
| *Individualised Aromas:** | | | |
| 5. MECHANICAL | | | |
| harsh, runny, fat, lithe,<br>marrowy, velvety, lean | | | |
| 6. COMMON CHEMICAL | | | |
| metallic, astringent, burning,<br>prickly, foreign* | | | |
| 7. FLAVOUR<br>(Olfacto-gustatory impression) | | | |
| flowery, fruity, herbacious,<br>common (not elegant), band,<br>earthy: marked or not | | | |

* Specify the nature of these when possible

# APPLE SCORING SHEET

Name

| STIMULATION PRIOR TO TASTING | IDENTIFICATION | INTENSITY | QUALITY |
|---|---|---|---|
| 1. VISUAL | | | |
| *Form:* spherical, elongated, flattened | | | |
| *Colour:* green, yellow, yellowish orange, brown, red, speckled, uniform | | | |
| *Appearance:* waxy, rough, smooth, shiny, flat, spotted | | | |
| 2. OLFACTORY | | | |
| weak, pronounced, very pronounced | | | |
| STIMULATIONS DURING TASTING | | | |
| 3. AUDITORY | | | |
| crisp | | | |
| 4. MECHANICAL | | | |
| granular, firm, chewy juiciness | | | |
| *Mastication:* resistance: weak, noticeable | | | |
| 5. GUSTATORY | | | |
| sweet, acid, bitter, salty | | | |
| 6. OLFACTO-GUSTATORY FLAVOUR | | | |
| pleasant, unpleasant | | | |
| 7. COMMON CHEMICAL | | | |
| presence or absence | | | |
| OBSERVATION UPON PEELING | | | |

# BASIC SCORING SHEET

| Name | IDENTIFICATION | INTENSITY 0-10 | QUALITY −5· +5 |
|---|---|---|---|
| STIMULATION PRIOR TO TASTING | | | |
| 1. VISUAL | | | |
| *Form:* | | | |
| *Colour:* | | | |
| *Appearance:* viscous, unctuous, crystalline, opalescent, fluorescent, phosphorescent, $CO_2$ clear, cloudy, alveolate or pitted, oily, porous | | | |
| 2. OLFACTORY | | | |
| aggregate odours<br>individualised aromas | | | |
| STIMULATIONS DURING TASTING | | | |
| 3. GUSTATORY | | | |
| sweet, salty, acid, bitter | | | |
| 4. FLAVOUR | | | |
| gustatory + olfactory | | | |
| 5. COMMON CHEMICAL | | | |
| metallic, astringent, burning, prickling | | | |
| 6. MECHANICAL | | | |
| unctuous, juicy, granular, elastic, hard, dried out | | | |
| mastication | | | |
| 7. THERMAL | | | |
| cold, hot | | | |
| 8. AUDITORY | | | |
| crunchy, crisp, brittle, friable | | | |

# FIGURE A: DESCRIPTIVE ANALYSIS EVALUATION TABLE LAYOUT

In front of each judge/taster are four wines which will be evaluated by descriptive analysis.

In the centre of the table are ten glasses. A control wine (unadulterated) is located at each end.

All other numbered glasses are the same wine – but have a 'standard' (component) added.

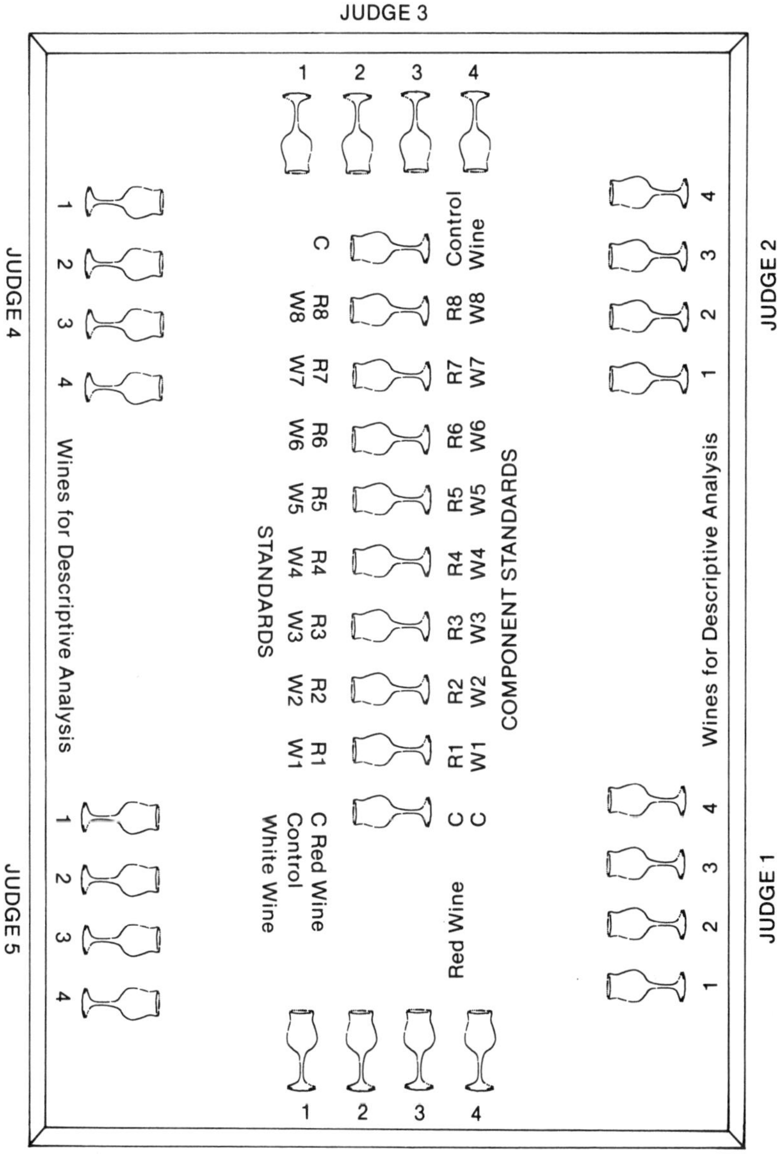

## SIGHT

| | | |
|---|---|---|
| 4 | Excellent | *Brilliant* with outstanding characteristic colour |
| 3 | Good | Bright with characteristic colour |
| 2 | Average | Clear, without obvious faults |
| 1 | Poor | Dull or slightly off colour |
| 0 | Objectionable | Cloudy and off colour |

*(See chapter 2)*

## SCORES

| | |
|---|---|
| 18-20 | Extraordinary |
| 15-17 | Excellent |
| 12-14 | Good |
| 9-11 | Pleasant |
| 6- 8 | Acceptable |
| 0- 5 | Poor and objectionable |

## NOTES

Break up points into ¼s, ½s or ¾s –
leave the perfect *full* score for
the wine that's unbeatable

As this record can be used with any wine style or grape variety it is helpful to have guidance to the *style* or wine *type*, eg Champagne, Chardonnay, Sherry.

## IN MOUTH – TACTILE – TASTE

| | | |
|---|---|---|
| 6 | Extraordinary | Unmistakable characteristic *flavour* of a grape variety or wine type. Extraordinary balance. Smooth, full-bodied, mouth-filling and overhwhelming. |
| 5 | Excellent | All of the above but a little less. Excellent but not overwhelming. |
| 4 | Good | Characteristic grape variety or wine type flavour. Good *balance*. Smooth. May have minor faults. Good wine. |
| 3 | Pleasant | Undistinguished wine but pleasant. |
| 2 | Acceptable | Undistinguished wine with minor imperfections and/or more pronounced faults than 5, 4 or 3 above. |
| 1 | Poor | Offensive flavours. May be drinable with strong foods. |
| 0 | Objectionable | Undrinkable. |

*(See chapter 4)*

## AROMA AND BOUQUET

| | | |
|---|---|---|
| 6 | Extraordinary | Unmistakable characteristic *aroma* of grape variety or wine type. Outstanding and complex *bouquet*. Exceptional *balance* or aroma bouquet. |
| 5 | Excellent | Characteristic aroma. Complex bouquet. Well balanced. |
| 4 | Good | Characteristic aroma. Distinguishable bouquet. |
| 3 | Pleasant | Slight aroma and bouquet, but pleasant. |
| 2 | Acceptable | No perceptable aroma or bouquet or 6, 5 or 4 above with slight off odours. |
| 1 | Poor | Rating 3 above with slight off odours. |
| 0 | Objectionable and offensive off odours. | |

*(See chapter 3)*

NATIONAL ACADEMY

WINE EVALUATION RECORD

Occasion L'[illegible] DuVin Place ST. LOUIS Date 30/5/85

| WINE RIESLINGS | PRICE | SIGHT 4 MAX | [AR]OMA/ [BO]UQUET [6] MAX | IN MOUTH 6 MAX | FINISH 2 MAX | OVERALL 2 MAX | TOTAL 20 MAX | IDEAL FOOD PAIRING |
|---|---|---|---|---|---|---|---|---|
| [illegible]T. JEAN | SV | 3.75 | 5.00 | 5.00 | 1.75 | 2.00 | 17.50 | BASKET CHICKEN |
| MONDAVI RIESLING | NV | 3.7[illegible] | 3.25 | 5.00 | 1.75 | 2.00 | 17.75 | SHRIMP, BEAN SALAD |
| [illegible]LL RIESLING | M | 3.75 | 5.00 | 4.75 | 1.50 | 1.50 | 16.50 | ASPARAGUS |
| [illegible]REY VINEYARD | M | 3.75 | 4.75 | 5.00 | 1.75 | 1.50 | 16.75 | COLD CHICKEN |
| [illegible]REGOR | NY | 3.7 | [illegible].50 | 5.25 | 2.00 | 2.00 | 18.50 | CLAM CHOWDER |

| FINISH | | |
|---|---|---|
| 2 | Excellent | Lingering outstanding aftertaste. |
| 1 | Good | Pleasant aftertaste. |
| 0 | Poor | Little or no distinguishable aftertaste. Unpleasant aftertaste. |

| *OVERALL* | |
|---|---|
| 2 | Excellent |
| 1 | Good |
| 0 | Poor |

(An opportunity to give bonus points)

Attention: Remember to look for the good features of each wine rather than the bad.

# DESCRIPTIVE ANALYSIS

The aim of this book has been to stress the individuality of wine and food lovers, and encourage them not to follow the pack. Each person seeks different flavours, has individual sensory perceptions. Competition judges seek winners of the various classes or categories and, as a rule, arrive at what we consider worthwhile judgements, regardless of where, when or how these judgements were made.

Aside from these competitions, the winelover should seek wines he or she personally prefers and should not be influenced by competition results; events that were staged at another place at another time, from another bottle, by another group of people. No result can be anything other than from this bottle at this place, at this time, by this group or person.

This book has provided many exercises (which I hope you have undertaken) so that you can understand and measure your personal sensory perceptions and thresholds for touch, smell and taste. As a result, you should now be able to recognise the many components of wine you like or dislike, and be able to quantify these hedonic pleasures. Having gained this knowledge, you will be able to make positive and qualified choices of preferred wines. Hence, your main purpose in evaluating wines will be to select your preferred wines.

In my sensory evaluation seminars I endeavour to teach, not which wine is best (a subject of personal interest only), but rather how four similar wines, from the same grape variety, are different. These wines can be four cabernets, chardonnays, rieslings, pinot noirs or zinfandels. They may all come from the same district or four different countries; but why are they different? My sensory evaluation seminars conclude with the following descriptive analysis and in-mouth profiling exercises. These will bring you to 'concert pitch'. Do not think that doing this on one occasion will be any great salvation; it won't! But it will open the door to a new experience, a truly professional experience. I have participated in these exercises many hundred times and still learn much on every occasion. Remember that training our senses is similar to training our muscles and mind – practise makes perfect!

These exercises were introduced to me by Dr A.C. Noble, so I will let her explain what they are all about. The following article appeared in the *American Wine Society Journal:*

*The big difference between descriptive analysis and quality rating lies in the objective, analytical, specific terminology employed in the former approach versus the hedonic, evaluative and judgemental assessment of the latter. The primary problem which arises in the use of quality scorecards is that it is a judgement based on overall perception. Since quality is a composite response to the sensory properties of the wine, based on our expectations which have developed from our previous experiences with a wide range of wines and our own personal preferences, this judgement is an individual response. No two people integrate the individual attributes in the same way, much less have the same preferences.*

*Two simple examples can illustrate this. Presented with a generic Californian red wine with 1-2 per cent sugar and a dry cabernet sauvignon, most wine drinkers claim to prefer the latter (although an enormous market exists for the former wine type). Using 'expert judges' to rate quality of these two wines may result in their being scored 12 and 17 on the Davis 20 point scorecard, but only by a more descriptive approach can the wines be meaningfully differentiated. One has to know the preferences of the judges to even guess which wine was given the 17!*

*In the second example, when presented with Californian chardonnays and asked to pick the higher quality wine, five experts chose wine A and five chose wine B. The conclusion is not that the wines are not different, but that the experts had different quality assessments and preferences. By a descriptive approach, we learn that wine A has an intense oak aroma and very little fruit, whereas wine B is characterised by apricot, apple and honey notes, with some vanilla.*

*The major requirements for terms used in descriptive evaluation of wine is that the terms be specific and capable of being defined. Clearly, subjective hedonic nomenclature does not meet this criterion, since such terms usually have a different meaning to each individual. 'Apricot', 'vanilla' and 'black pepper' are specific terms which can be defined unequivocally with physical standards. In contrast 'rich', 'good nose', 'vinous', 'middle-roundness', 'high-tonality' are vague and imprecise adjectives, which cannot be understood by others without extensive discussion, if at all!*

While this exercise can be performed solo, it's quite easy to set up for five, 10 or 20 people as it is for one. You can try the exercise with 8-10 standards or modify it to have only 3-4 standards.

For the 8 point profile we need a jug or flagon commercial red or white wine, preferably bland (for the standards), and a few sniff sticks.

Pour one to one and a half ounces into each of 10 glasses. Mark the foot of each glass with a felt pen, the first and last glass in the lineup is marked with C to indicate 'control' wine. Number the remaining glasses 1 through 8 and prefix with R for red wine or W for white wine. Add the following components to the glasses with a sniff stick:

| For white wine evaluation | For red wine evaluation |
|---|---|
| Glass W1 Ethyl Acetate | Glass R1 Ethyl Acetate |
| Glass W2 Diacetyl | Glass R2 Diacetyl |
| Glass W3 Sulphur Dioxide | Glass R3 Bell Pepper/Capsicum/Asparagus |
| Glass W4 Linalool | Glass R4 Berry |
| Glass W5 Citrus | Glass R5 Raisin |
| Glass W6 Fruity/Apricot | Glass R6 Black Pepper |
| Glass W7 Floral | Glass R7 Vanilla |
| Glass W8 Acetaldehyde | Glass R8 Soy |

Do not wet more that 1/8th of an inch of the sniff stick with the component as many of them are really potent (linalool, floral and apricot in particular). Some components may need a double dose, that's a personal choice. To improve your threshold, try decreasing the amount each time you do the exercise.

You can chop up fresh bell pepper and raisins as alternatives for R3 and R5, or use fresh lemon juice for W5, and apricot puree for W6. Other options are listed on the 'spider' profiles. All you need is a little imagination and almost any wine odour can be simulated.

## PROCEDURE

Prepare the standards and set them in the centre of the table (Fig A). Each judge has 4-6 wines to be evaluated in the glasses in front of them, and each judge will require an evaluation 'spider web' sheet with sufficient points to cover the number of standards. Each of the standards glasses should be covered with a numbered petrie dish lid, saucer or other suitable cover, so that the room doesn't smell like a perfume factory, nor the judges become confused by the conglomeration of smells.

Prior to smelling any glass, the lid should be held firmly on the glass, then the glass rotated or shaken. The glass should be taken to the nose before removing the lid otherwise a lot of the odour will dissipate.

Each person should smell the control wine to commence the exercise, then smell a numbered standard. Having memorised this component, the judge then smells the wines to be evaluated to determine, on a scale of 10, how much of that particular component is in the four wines, and then marks this intensity with an X on that particular 'spoke'.

So, if your first standard is R2, you would mark the 'diacetyl' spoke with an X representing the intensity you gauged for each wine. Perhaps you could mark the intensity with the number of the wine judged, numbering 1-4 from the left. (See Fig B). Now, smell the control wine again (do this before you smell each standard) and try another standard, this time maybe the next one will be R1, ethyl acetate. Repeat the above procedure, marking the intensity of ethyl acetate in each of your four wines. Next, join up the two spokes with coloured pencils or coded lines (See Fig C).

## FIGURE B: MARK THE INTENSITY

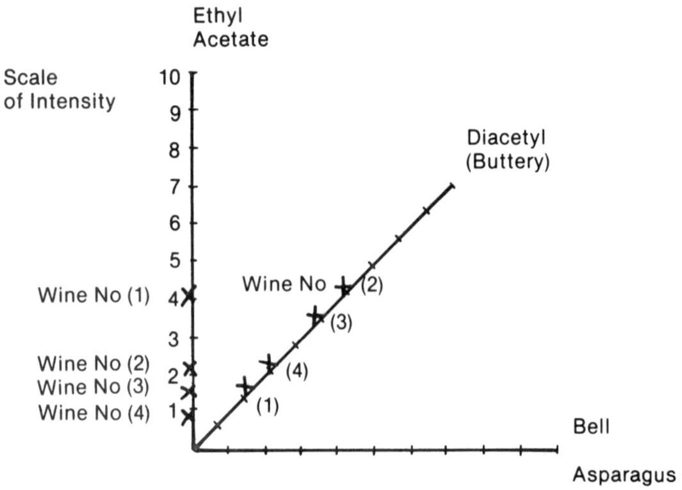

# FIGURE C: JOIN THE X'S

Now – join up the numbers or x's with colour pencils or codes, ie
Wine 1 ...........
Wine 2 ------------
Wine 3 ·x·x·x·x·x·x
Wine 4 ·o·o·o·o·o·o

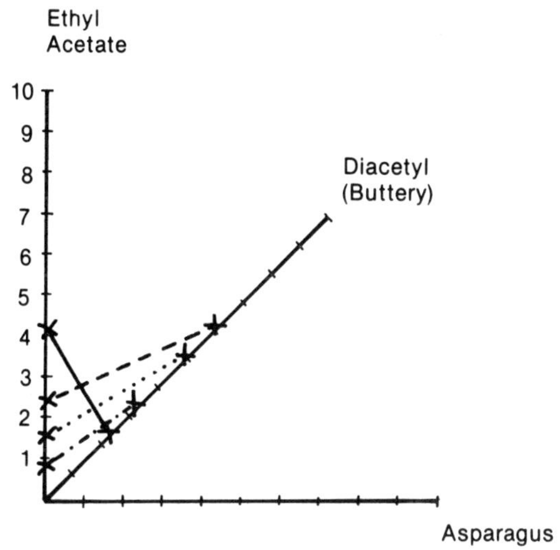


Now proceed to measure the intensity of each of the standards, remembering to:

1. Swirl each glass with the lid held firmly on until you bring the glass to your nose.
2. Smell the control wine before each standard.
3. Mark your colour code at the bottom of your sheet.

Early in your smelling career this exercise will quickly fatigue your olfactory receptors. Should you suffer smell fatigue, smell a glass of water and, if necessary, leave the room and go for a walk. When evaluating your four wines, while smelling it helps if you close your eyes.

Let's try to put it all together on an eight point profile with four cabernets from one region and find out how they are different.

This eight point profile tells us that:

Wine No. 1 ———— had significant amounts of ethyl acetate (vinegary smell), low in diacetyl and bell pepper, strong berry nose and in-mouth flavour, low black pepper and astringency.

Wine No. 2 ———— was lower in ethyl acetate, bell pepper, vegetative by mouth and astringency, but higher in black pepper, and berry in-mouth.

Wine No. 3 ·············· in fact, both wines 3 and 4 had more vegetative characters in the smell and in-mouth flavour. Wine 3 also had lots of black pepper on the nose.

Wine No 4 –·–·–·–·–·–· had tons of vegetative characters and astringency, but low in ethyl acetate and black pepper.

# DESCRIPTIVE ANALYSIS CABERNET, ZINFANDEL, PINOT NOIR, OR SYRAH PROFILE

1. SWIRL the wine in each and every glass prior to smelling.
2. PLOT the intensities scored for each wine, 0 – none, 10 – high, using an X.
3. JOIN UP the points using a different colour or code, eg ........, ------, ·x·x·x·x· or ———.
4. Be sure to record the colour or code below.

EIGHT POINT PROFILE OF FOUR CABERNETS FROM ONE REGION

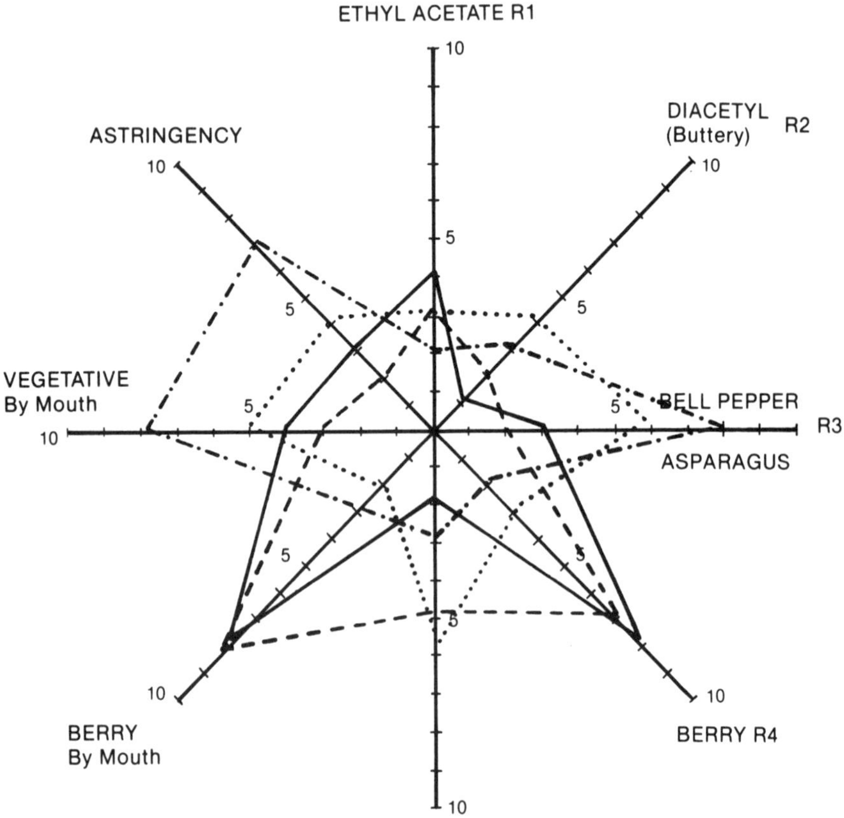


OPTIONS:
Raisin R5
Vanilla R7
Soy R8

Wine 1 ——— 2 - - - - - 3 ......... 4 —·—·—
or 1 ——— 2 - - - - - 3 ......... 4 —·—·—
(if colored pencils are unavailable)

# TELLING THE WORLD WHAT YOU THINK!

*(or articulating your impressions!)*

The time has come to put your words where your wine was.

If you have followed the summaries of each chapter, filled in your hedonic wine evaluation record and completed your descriptive analysis sheet, you are now equipped to stand up and speak about any wine in a totally obejctive and intelligent manner. But above all, in non-jargon, easily understood, descriptive terms.

Not only will you be articulate and cover every point, but you will be using words that are understood in Austin, Niagara Falls, Hong Kong, Auckland or Adelaide.

You have been asked to describe a typical young red wine, for example a chambourcin from Ohio or a cabernet from California or the Barossa. Try this formula:

SIGHT

Colour – intense deep red with the colour extending to the very edge of the tongue; no watery rim.

Appearance – star bright to brilliant, indicating a wine of high acidity. I've given it 3.75/4.00 for sight.

OLFACTORY – SMELL

Aroma – Distinctly varietal, as I understand this variety. There is a strong and pleasant berry aroma which tells me that the wine has been made from ripe fruit. I expect the wine to have a lot of fruit when I come to the in-mouth appraisal. Bouquet – Slight $SO_2$ evident, tickles the upper reaches of the nose – alcohol is high enough to be perceived in the nasal passage. I have no objection about either of these components in a young red wine. To my threshold, the oak is also pronounced, but I believe this will marry with all the fruit and alcohol. I also perceived a small amount of volatile acidity, but then again I have a low threshold for VA. I think this adds to the complexity of the wine.

All these components would portend a lively, mouth-filling wine. I scored it at 4.75/6.00 for nose.

IN-MOUTH

Having rolled the wine around in my mouth, chewed it, and retained it long enough to allow the wine to warm in my mouth, the first impression confirms my external sight and smell judgements. It certainly is a mouthful of wine, lots of ripe berry fruit, the $SO_2$ is slightly drying on the roof of the mouth and the touch of volatility helps the smell appraisal.

Tactile – The obvious viscosity confirms the alcohol, I would estimate about 12½-13 per cent, the grape and wood tannins certainly fill up the mouth from the teeth to the throat, and help make this a very complex wine. The grape tannin is moderately aggressive at this young age but will round out as the wine evolves through bottle maturation.

Taste – The acidity that was obvious from the brilliant appearance is evident on the teeth and tongue. In my opinion, this wine is a very good long term cellaring wine, eight years plus. I also appreciae the slightly perceivable bitterness at the back of the mouth. Being a young wine the acids and tannins are astringent and out of balance, but these along with the abundant berry fruit are what I think makes it such a good cellaring wine. My score for the in-mouth evaluation 4.50/6.00. After taste 1.75 and 1.75 extra for the overall impression, making a total of 16.5 out of 20.

## DESCRIPTORS IN COMMON USE FOR VARIETAL WINES

*Syrah, Shiraz, Petite Syrah:* Black pepper, coffee grounds and soy in older wines, Berry (blackberry/mulberry) spicy, dried fruit (raisiny).

*Pinot Noir:* Berry (raspberry/strawberry), cherry, cinnamon, mint.

*Cabernet Sauvignon, Cabernet Franc, Malbec, Merlot:* Berry fruit, capsicum/ green pepper, black olives, asparagus (vegetable), mint, vanilla, cassis, cigar box (cedar), spicy, herbaceous, eucalyptus.

*Zinfandel:* Berry, artificial fruit, raisins, soy, black pepper, vanilla.

*Chardonnay:* Buttery, a wide range of fruit flavours including green apple, grapefruit, melon, pineapple, citrus, stone fruit – peach, apricot, nectarine – oak, floral, fig, butterscotch and vanilla (from oak).

*Riesling (Johanisberg, Rhine):* Flora, estery, fruity – citrus lemon/lime, – spicy, fresh, kerosene – with age, toasty, geranium, clove, confectionary.

*Chenin blanc:* Pineapple juice, apple, lemon, curry.

*Gewurztraminer:* Lychee, tropical fruit salad, spicy, curry, ginger, apricot, perfumed soap, earthy.

*Sauvignon blanc:* Grassy, herbaceous, tin peas, floral, citrus, stone fruit, vegetative: asparagus, green pepper/capcisum, gooseberry.

HAG

# INDEX

The author and publisher wish to acknowledge the following organisations and publishers for permission to use their materials. Macbeth, a division of Kollmorgen Corporation, Newburgh, New York for material included in chapter 2; *Decanter Magazine* Limited, 31-33 High Holborn, London WC1V 6AW, for extract on p. 107; *American Wine Society Journal* for quote on p. 120; the American Society for Enology and Viticulture for Aroma Wheel on p. 55.

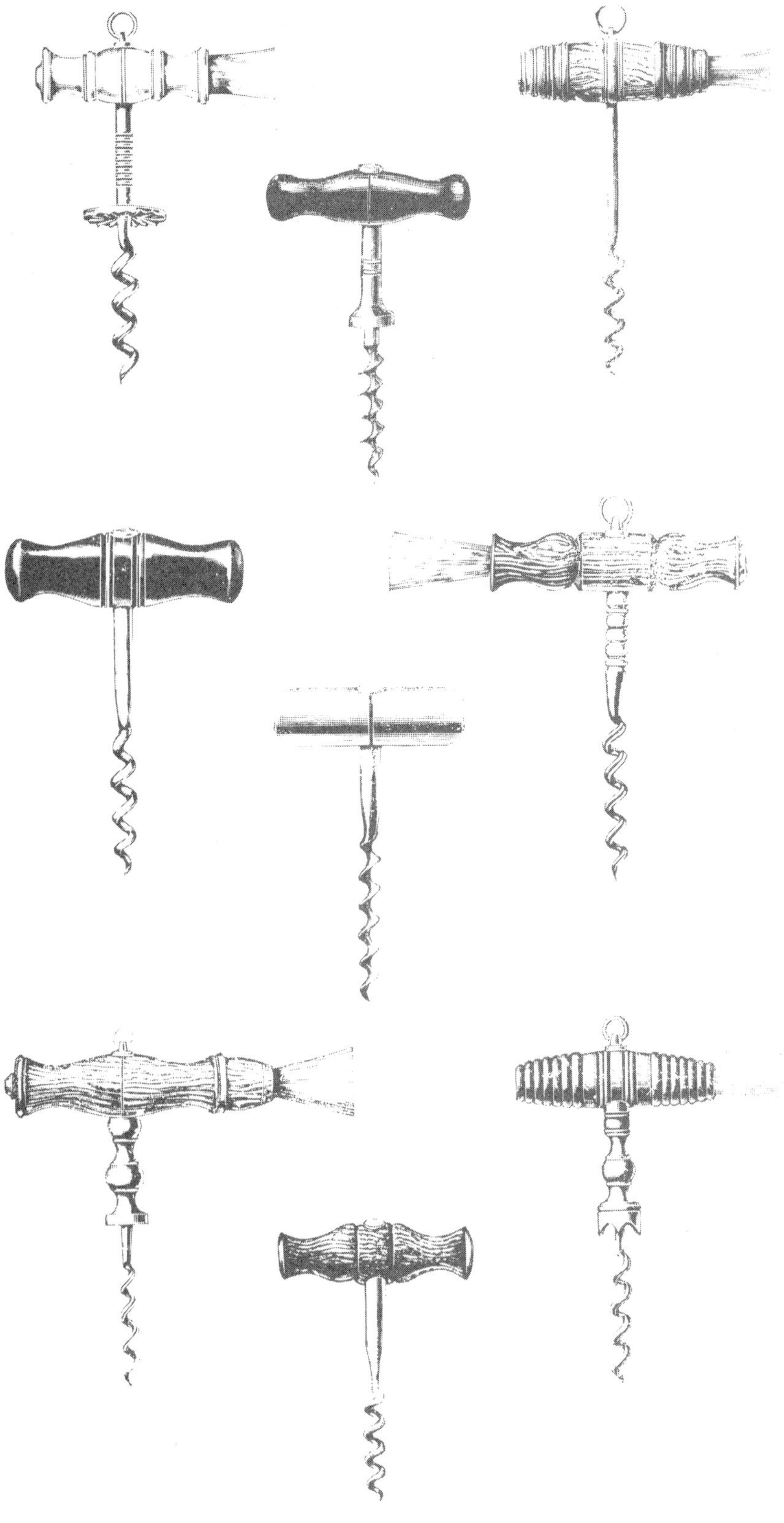